THE COMPLETE MANUAL OF OCCULT DIVINATION

The Book of Destiny, Volume II

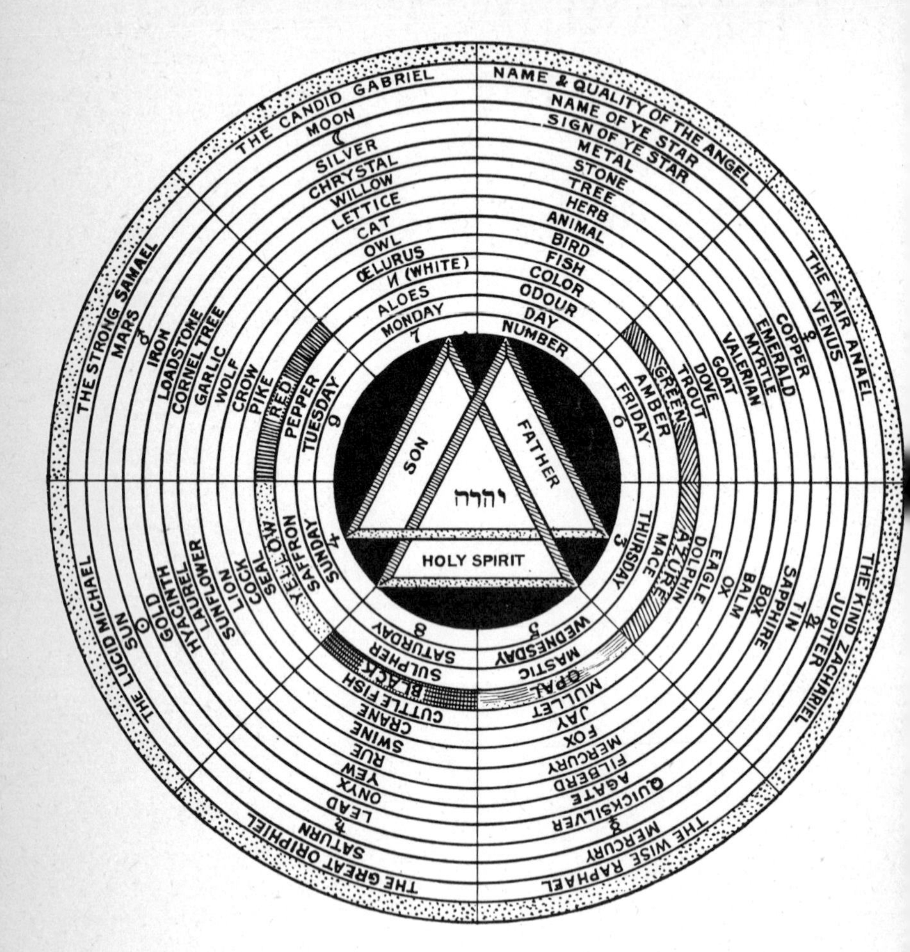

THE WHEEL OF WISDOM.

The Complete Manual of Occult Divination

The Book of Destiny

Volume II

by

GRAND ORIENT (A. E. WAITE)

Introduction by

LESLIE SHEPARD

UNIVERSITY BOOKS, INC. NEW HYDE PARK, N.Y. 11040

Library of Congress Catalog Card Number: 78-118598

Manufactured in the United States of America

Printed in U.S.A. by
NOBLE OFFSET PRINTERS, INC.
NEW YORK 3, N. Y.

CONTENTS

PREFACE

IF the workings of that which is called Fate or Destiny were not beyond calculation in respect of diversity, one would say that the modes of reading therein were making a bid for recognition on the score of equal variation in kind, aspect and degree. So numerous indeed are they that after many years of research and collation I have not reached to the end of them and am even now coming upon things rare and strange, apart from mere curiosities which appeal to the collector only. I know also that beyond the records in occult literature there is all that which never passes into writing, because every intuitive man and woman who exercises the gifts of seership will in the course of time develop a personal method which serves in his or her particular case, and in this way the arts of fortune-telling are not less numerous than the artists. I do not propose to establish a criterion of value by affirming that such individual processes are the only matters of moment in the whole subject: all personal divination has been suggested by and developed from that which has been made current in books, and after we have isolated the products of common colportage, with other negligible devices which swarm in the byways, the fact remains that there is much which has come down to us from the past and is not without authority, once the hypothesis is granted that the future can be discovered and that there is something in the law of life which corresponds to the idea of destiny. It is on these that seership has worked from time immemorial; it is these that must be taken at the present day by all who would develop the gift and find how it operates in them. They also will end by working out, almost insensibly, a method which is in a sense peculiar to themselves, though it may be and will be in the likeness of much that has preceded. Herein lies the office of good books on the subject, and their worth or authority resides in the fact that all devices are pretexts for awaking and developing that which resides in our own nature—a faculty of catholic intuition which can and does on occasion seem to overcome the limitations created by time and space.

In *A Manual of Cartomancy, Fortune-Telling and Occult Divination,* I gave some prominence to this view of the subject, and the collection is now in its fifth and largest edition, revised—as I think—finally and much extended in material. With those things of the art which have a claim to be called serious, after their own manner, I interblended some which were matters of diversion only, so that readers who happen to have no psychic powers—because they have omitted to develop them—might not find the ingarnering altogether beyond their purpose. I remarked also that for others who are born seers, even the arbitrary and automatic processes will not be without result. I ventured also in a few sections—such as *The Book of the Secret Word* and *The Art of Ruling by the Law of Grace*—to indicate that there was and remains a higher side of the whole subject. The success of the work is referable in a very large measure to these facts, and I have followed the same rule in the present collection. *The Great Oracle of the Gods* can be used merely as an amusing game of chance, or, by the psychic interpretation of its great sheaf of oracular responses, it can be turned into a prolific method of divining. *The Art of Knowing the Good Genii* is a section of the Practical Kabalah in its root-matter and was first rendered out of Hebrew into the Latin tongue, somewhere in the seventeenth century, by the Jesuit Athanasius Kircher. It is therefore a matter of tradition and it is difficult to speak of its antiquity, but the elements are exceedingly old. In the final section of this art I have shewn after what manner the consideration of the Hebrew angelical hierarchy can be exalted into the realm of mystical research, even into mystic practice for the opening of the world of Grace, the world of Divine Knowledge, in the soul of the prepared student. Debased Kabalism turned these things into the monstrous observances which are denominated Black Magic, but in their proper understanding they belong to God. As a further illustration of this truth, I have taken a bolder course in *The Wheel of Wisdom.* It is based upon a rare manuscript, which once belonged to Dr Ebenezer Sibly, an astrological antiquary of the eighteenth century. I have purged it of corrupt elements and have restored it to its proper place in the spiritual side of its subject.

The other methods may be left to speak for themselves at their proper value, but there is one word in conclusion. Destiny is the course of events which is followed by those who are content to go with the tide : we can adapt our own destiny. That which we call accident is that which is put into our hands, to be shaped by us and in us. The things that are denominated fatalities, by which a definite term is put to our activity in certain directions, are better known and understood as interventions of God in the order of human things. These are also put into our hands, if we have truly eyes to see. Even the fatality of sudden and unprovided death belongs to this category, because the present manifest order is then succeeded by another, to which we are transferred thenceforward, and life is still in our hands. I take it that those who accept this ruling will not be likely to suppose that we can read the future and our chance or destiny therein by the help of any arbitrary process. But those who have eyes can see in the glass of vision, and sometimes anything for them will serve as a pretext. To such as these I would say that all prevision or forecast lies within its own circle and the soul which is dedicated to Divine Ends has no real part therein. This *Book of Destiny* is therefore for those whom it concerns in the lesser ways. I deserve well of my readers if I have tried here and there to get them out of the imputed circle of necessity into another world of vision. In 1920 I may have something to tell them of Destiny and the Art of Reading therein which has never been put into language. But the time is not yet. It remains to be said that no divinatory process and no process of fortune-telling, unless utterly brief and simple, can be practised successfully without reasonable care and attention on the part of the student, so that the principle of the particular system may be mastered before proceeding to work. There is another point. All answers are subject to certain necessary modifications, though they call only for the use of common-sense. Some presuppose that the Querent or the person by or for whom the inquiry is made belongs to the male sex, but the actual Querent or person may be female. Some answers speak of matters in the plural, and they may need to be adjusted to the singular. Above and beyond details of this kind, there is the lawful modification of answers in so far as their method of expression is manifestly inapplicable to a case in view; but this must, of course, be done so that the spirit of the Oracle remains unaltered. For example, Question 45 in *The Great Oracle of the Gods* reads: "Is the person dead about whom we are anxious?" The answer obtained may be of a direct kind. If *The Court of Fortune* has produced the Number 5, then, following the rule of the system, it will be found on p. 41—XX. THEMIS, 5—and will read: "He has died bravely." But if the Number 9 has been obtained, it will be found on p. 46—XXIV. LATONA, 9—and will read: "You would be sorry to know the truth about the life he is leading." This tells you that your anxiety is misplaced, for the person in question is alive; but you have grave cause for solicitude in another respect than you had anticipated. This is a simple instance of reading between the lines of the Oracle, not—as the saying is—to trick the proper meaning, but to elicit its inward sense.

GRAND ORIENT.

THE GREAT ORACLE OF THE GODS

CALLED ALSO

THE BOOK OF THE SPEECH OF HERMES-MERCURIUS AND THE TRUE WHEEL OF FORTUNE

OF THE HOUSES OF FORTUNE

THE Houses of Fortune are many and the methods of exploring their mysteries with the object of deciding beforehand the destinies of human beings exceed numeration. Some of them are modern inventions and most of these rank only as properties belonging to the common theatre of jugglery. Others have at least the merit of a certain antiquity, and *The Great Oracle of the Gods* is entitled to consideration on this score, for it first came to light in the French language nearly two hundred years ago. Its age is not, however, its only title, for it seems to me one of the most ingenious compilations which I have met with in the course of my researches, on the understanding, however, that its oracles—on the surface at least—are those of chance and not of divination in the proper sense of the term. Unless he chooses to exercise the art of interpretation on the responses themselves, they demand no gifts of seership on the part of the Querent: they demand, furthermore, no Operator but himself, and the method is simplicity itself, so that the beginner can scarcely err therein. Finally, the Oracle is here made known for the first time and will doubtless rank as an interesting addition to the English literature of Fortune-telling.

QUESTIONS DETERMINED BY THE GODS WHO PRESIDE OVER THE WHEEL OF FORTUNE

1. The destiny of the newly born child.
2. Whether the child will live and grow up.
3. Whether he will enter the Church.
4. Whether he will have a reversion.
5. What he will be like in the future.
6. Whether he will persevere in the calling chosen by him.
7. Whether he will be happy under a master.
8. Whether he will be a person of consideration in the calling adopted by him.
9. The way to get on.
10. What success is awaiting the enterprise?
11. How will the persons turn out who have been chosen in this matter?
12. Whether the person in view will continue in his present business?
13. What do the persons concerned think of the end of the matter?

14. What fortune will follow in this case a change of condition and state ?

15. Whether I shall continue till death in my present business.

16. Shall I attain that which I now desire ?

17. Which of the persons in view is the most ambitious ?

18. Will the proposed business prove advantageous ?

19. Does the person now in my mind detest me ?

20. Shall I gain this advantage ?

21. Is the current rumour reliable ?

22. How will my present inclination, affection, or love end ?

23. Will that happen which I have now in my mind ?

24. Are my friends faithful ?

25. The character of the person in my mind.

26. Shall I marry soon ?

27. Will a certain marriage be fortunate ?

28. Shall I marry the person now in my thoughts ?

29. What fortune will follow the marriage ?

30. What will be the disposition of the husband ?

31. What will be the wife's disposition ?

32. How many times shall I marry ?

33. Shall I have children ?

34. Will the expected child be a girl or boy ?

35. Will the husband outlive the wife, or *vice versa* ?

36. What is the ground of divorce ?
37. Will the widow remarry ?
38. Will the year prove prosperous ?
39. To whom shall I look for assistance ?
40. Shall I come into an inheritance ?
41. Will the business be profitable ?
42. In what country am I likely to make a fortune ?
43. Shall I succeed in the army ?
44. Will the traveller return shortly ?
45. Is the person dead about whom we are anxious ?
46. What is being said and done by the absent person ?
47. Which day of the week will be fortunate in my case ?
48. Shall I be lucky at games of chance ?
49. Shall I win the lawsuit ?
50. Is this a true dream ?
51. Shall I find that which I have lost ?
52. Is the person now in my mind able to keep a secret ?
53. Who is the thief in the present instance ?
54. How will the servant turn out who is now in my mind ?
55. Has he been to the tavern ?
56. Will the sick person recover ?
57. What will be the manner of my death ?
58. Shall I die rich ?
59. In what country shall I die ?
60. Is the person still in possession of that which can only be lost once ?

THE COURT OF FORTUNE

12	2	9	4	11	3
1	7	5	10	7	6
8	4	1	3	12	2
5	11	6	10	7	9
12	4	1	7	11	3
2	9	5	10	6	8
11	1	12	5	9	3
2	10	4	8	6	7
10	5	7	3	1	8
4	11	2	9	12	6

THE METHOD OF USING THE ORACLE

Those who have in their possession the fifth and most recent edition of *A Manual of Cartomancy* will be acquainted with the mode of consulting that New Oracle which is called *The Heart's Desire,* and they should refer to it at this point, because it is similar in several respects to the present method. It is indeed an old and widely prevailing device for certain kinds of Divination, and in the time-honoured process of Bibliomancy it was called the Practice of the Golden Stiletto. I will simplify it in the present instance, so as to make reference unnecessary on the part of any who are strangers to my previous volume.

Take a Stiletto, or at need any large needle. The consultation of THE GREAT ORACLE OF THE GODS begins by closing the eyes, concentrating the whole mind on the Question proposed to the Oracle and allowing the steel instrument, as it is held in the right hand, to indicate automatically one of the numbers contained in the 60 mystic squares of the COURT OF FORTUNE. The Stiletto must move by the power of your own magnetism, if you happen to be a magnetic subject, and if not you must pierce at random, keeping the eyes shut. The number must never be selected by your own eyes and will.

The number which you obtain in this manner will represent one of the 12 Chains of

Fortune in the list which follows hereafter, beginning with *Fortuna Prima* and ending with *Fortuna Duodecima.* In the Chain corresponding with the number obtained you will find the number of your Question, as you have selected it from the *Questions determined by the Gods,* enumerated in the previous list. The number of your Question will be on the left side of the Chain, preceding the name of the God who will provide the answer. On the right side will be found the number of the Oracle in Roman figures. Turn to that figure in the *Answers of the Gods* and against the Gothic number which you obtained in the *Court of Fortune,* you will find the decision of the Oracle.

The method of finding is really of the utmost simplicity, but I will illustrate it by two examples, taken at random.

EXAMPLE I.—I am anxious for an answer to Question 15 in the *Questions determined by the Gods.* I refer to *The Court of Fortune,* take the Stiletto in my hand, hold it over the Magic Square of Numbers which constitutes the Court, close my eyes, and presently it indicates—let us say—the No. 6 in the Square. I turn to *Fortuna Sexta* in *The Twelve Aspects of the Oracle* and look for the No. 15, being that of my Question. I find against it: ACHILLES LI. I turn to the Oracle of Achilles, who is God 51, in *The Answers of the Gods.* I consult line 6, because 6 is the number given me in the *Court of Fortune,* and I obtain the answer as follows : "You will die in harness, and you will remain in lasting memory."

EXAMPLE II.—I am seeking an answer to Question 5, or What I shall be like in the future ? I have drawn the No. 12 from *The Court of Fortune.* I refer to *Fortuna Duodecima.* I find the No. 5, which is that of my Question. It directs me to consult Vulcan VII. in *The Answers of the Gods.* I have recourse to that God and against the No. 12, which is that of the number given me by *The Court of Fortune,* I obtain the answer. It tells me that I shall have no special capacity for any kind of public service.

It will be observed that both Questions and answers are sometimes in the third person and sometimes in the first : They can all be read either way, so that the subject of inquiry can be adapted to your own requirements or to those of another for whom or about whom you are consulting the Oracle.

Moreover, *The Answers of the Gods* may be understood as Oracles and can then be checked by the characteristics attributed to each. Thus Hercules teaches you how to overcome all things, as stated in the description at the head of his Oracle, and if you search in yourself, you may find by his aid a means to insure what he promises, not only by zeal in business but in those ways which keep the just man in everlasting remembrance. On the other hand, the description of Vulcan bids you take care lest he soil you. This means that his Oracles are not to be taken of necessity as expressions of the mouth of truth. Again you must look in yourself, for it may be, although deep down, that you can evoke inactive qualities by which you may yet be fitted for the public service. So also in consultation for others, you can assist them to look in themselves, check the utterances of the Gods and perhaps find that which has been hidden even from the Querents themselves.

In this way, THE GREAT ORACLE OF THE GODS can be something more than a game of chance and a mere method of fortune-telling.

Begin by a careful study of the Examples here given and you will master the method quickly. The gift of wise interpretation should come later for those who require it.

FORTUNA PRIMA

Question.	Oracles.	Mystic No.	Question.	Oracles.	Mystic No.
1	Caro	LX	31	Satyrs	XXX
2	Rhadamanthus	LIX	32	Fauns	XXIX
3	Minos	LVIII	33	Nymphs	XXVIII
4	Prometheus	LVII	34	Muses	XXVII
5	Aristeus	LVI	35	Sibyls	XXVI
6	Æsculapius	LV	36	Feronia	XXV
7	Perseus	LIV	37	Latona	XXIV
8	Orpheus	LIII	38	Pomona	XXIII
9	Atlas	LII	39	Cybele	XXII
10	Achilles	LI	40	Flora	XXI
11	Hercules	L	41	Themis	XX
12	Theseus	XLIX	42	Minerva	XIX
13	Jason	XLVIII	43	Diana	XVIII
14	Janus	XLVII	44	Proserpine	XVII
15	Priapus	XLVI	45	Juno	XVI
16	Serapis	XLV	46	Bellona	XV
17	Momus	XLIV	47	Aurora	XIV
18	Æolus	XLIII	48	Venus	XIII
19	Cerberus	XLII	49	Ceres	XII
20	Furies	XLI	50	Vesta	XI
21	Lamiæ	XL	51	Mercury	X
22	Harpies	XXXIX	52	Apollo	IX
23	Syrens	XXXVIII	53	Pan	VIII
24	Giants	XXXVII	54	Vulcan	VII
25	Fates	XXXVI	55	Bacchus	VI
26	Genii	XXXV	56	Mars	V
27	Lares	XXXIV	57	Pluto	IV
28	Penates	XXXIII	58	Neptune	III
29	Centaurs	XXXII	59	Saturn	II
30	Tritons	XXXI	60	Jupiter	I

FORTUNA SECUNDA

Question.	Oracles.	Mystic No.	Question.	Oracles.	Mystic No.
1	Jupiter	I	31	Tritons	XXXI
2	Caro	LX	32	Satyrs	XXX
3	Rhadamanthus	LIX	33	Fauns	XXIX
4	Minos	LVIII	34	Nymphs	XXVIII
5	Prometheus	LVII	35	Muses	XXVII
6	Aristeus	LVI	36	Sibyls	XXVI
7	Æsculapius	LV	37	Feronia	XXV
8	Perseus	LIV	38	Latona	XXIV
9	Orpheus	LIII	39	Pomona	XXIII
10	Atlas	LII	40	Cybele	XXII
11	Achilles	LI	41	Flora	XXI
12	Hercules	L	42	Themis	XX
13	Theseus	XLIX	43	Minerva	XIX
14	Jason	XLVIII	44	Diana	XVIII
15	Janus	XLVII	45	Proserpine	XVII
16	Priapus	XLVI	46	Juno	XVI
17	Serapis	XLV	47	Bellona	XV
18	Momus	XLIV	48	Aurora	XIV
19	Æolus	XLIII	49	Venus	XIII
20	Cerberus	XLII	50	Ceres	XII
21	Furies	XLI	51	Vesta	XI
22	Lamiæ	XL	52	Mercury	X
23	Harpies	XXXIX	53	Apollo	IX
24	Syrens	XXXVIII	54	Pan	VIII
25	Giants	XXXVII	55	Vulcan	VII
26	Fates	XXXVI	56	Bacchus	VI
27	Genii	XXXV	57	Mars	V
28	Lares	XXXIV	58	Pluto	IV
29	Penates	XXXIII	59	Neptune	III
30	Centaurs	XXXII	60	Saturn	II

FORTUNA TERTIA

Question.	Oracles.	Mystic No.	Question.	Oracles.	Mystic No.
1	Saturn	II	31	Centaurs	XXXII
2	Jupiter	I	32	Tritons	XXXI
3	Charon	LX	33	Satyrs	XXX
4	Rhadamanthus	LIX	34	Fauns	XXIX
5	Minos	LVIII	35	Nymphs	XXVIII
6	Prometheus	LVII	36	Muses	XXVII
7	Aristeus	LVI	37	Sibyls	XXVI
8	Æsculapius	LV	38	Feronia	XXV
9	Perseus	LIV	39	Latona	XXIV
10	Orpheus	LIII	40	Pomona	XXIII
11	Atlas	LII	41	Cybele	XXII
12	Achilles	LI	42	Flora	XXI
13	Hercules	L	43	Themis	XX
14	Theseus	XLIX	44	Minerva	XIX
15	Jason	XLVIII	45	Diana	XVIII
16	Janus	XLVII	46	Proserpine	XVII
17	Priapus	XLVI	47	Juno	XVI
18	Serapis	XLV	48	Bellona	XV
19	Momus	XLIV	49	Aurora	XIV
20	Æolus	XLIII	50	Venus	XIII
21	Cerberus	XLII	51	Ceres	XII
22	Furies	XLI	52	Vesta	XI
23	Lamiæ	XL	53	Mercury	X
24	Harpies	XXXIX	54	Apollo	IX
25	Syrens	XXXVIII	55	Pan	VIII
26	Giants	XXXVII	56	Vulcan	VII
27	Fates	XXXVI	57	Bacchus	VI
28	Genii	XXXV	58	Mars	V
29	Lares	XXXIV	59	Pluto	IV
30	Penates	XXXIII	60	Neptune	III

FORTUNA QUARTA

Question.	Oracles.	Mystic No.	Question.	Oracles.	Mystic No.
1	Neptune	III	31	Penates	XXXIII
2	Saturn	II	32	Centaurs	XXXII
3	Jupiter	I	33	Tritons	XXXI
4	Charon	LX	34	Satyrs	XXX
5	Rhadamanthus	LIX	35	Fauns	XXIX
6	Minos	LVIII	36	Nymphs	XXVIII
7	Prometheus	LVII	37	Muses	XXVII
8	Aristeus	LVI	38	Sibyls	XXVI
9	Æsculapius	LV	39	Feronia	XXV
10	Perseus	LIV	40	Latona	XXIV
11	Orpheus	LIII	41	Pomona	XXIII
12	Atlas	LII	42	Cybele	XXII
13	Achilles	LI	43	Flora	XXI
14	Hercules	L	44	Themis	XX
15	Theseus	XLIX	45	Minerva	XIX
16	Jason	XLVIII	46	Diana	XVIII
17	Janus	LXVII	47	Proserpine	XVII
18	Priapus	XLVI	48	Juno	XVI
19	Serapis	XLV	49	Bellona	XV
20	Momus	XLIV	50	Aurora	XIV
21	Æolus	XLIII	51	Venus	XIII
22	Cerberus	XLII	52	Ceres	XII
23	Furies	XLI	53	Vesta	XI
24	Lamiæ	XL	54	Mercury	X
25	Harpies	XXXIX	55	Apollo	IX
26	Syrens	XXXVIII	56	Pan	VIII
27	Giants	XXXVII	57	Vulcan	VII
28	Fates	XXXVI	58	Bacchus	VI
29	Genii	XXXV	59	Mars	V
30	Lares	XXXIV	60	Pluto	IV

FORTUNA QUINTA

Question.	Oracles.	Mystic No.	Question.	Oracles.	Mystic No.
1	Pluto	IV	31	Lares	XXXIV
2	Neptune	III	32	Penates	XXXIII
3	Saturn	II	33	Centaurs	XXXII
4	Jupiter	I	34	Tritons	XXXI
5	Charon	LX	35	Satyrs	XXX
6	Rhadamanthus	LIX	36	Fauns	XXIX
7	Minos	LVIII	37	Nymphs	XXVIII
8	Prometheus	LVII	38	Muses	XXVII
9	Aristeus	LVI	39	Sibyls	XXVI
10	Æsculapius	LV	40	Feronia	XXV
11	Perseus	LIV	41	Latona	XXIV
12	Orpheus	LIII	42	Pomona	XXIII
13	Atlas	LII	43	Cybele	XXII
14	Achilles	LI	44	Flora	XXI
15	Hercules	L	45	Themis	XX
16	Theseus	XLIX	46	Minerva	XIX
17	Jason	XLVIII	47	Diana	XVIII
18	Janus	XLVII	48	Proserpine	XVII
19	Priapus	XLVI	49	Juno	XVI
20	Serapis	XLV	50	Bellona	XV
21	Momus	XLIV	51	Aurora	XIV
22	Æolus	XLIII	52	Venus	XIII
23	Cerberus	XLII	53	Ceres	XII
24	Furies	XLI	54	Vesta	XI
25	Lamiæ	XL	55	Mercury	X
26	Harpies	XXXIX	56	Apollo	IX
27	Syrens	XXXVIII	57	Pan	VIII
28	Giants	XXXVII	56	Vulcan	VII
29	Fates	XXXVI	59	Bacchus	VI
30	Genii	XXXV	60	Mars	V

FORTUNA SEXTA

Question.	Oracles.	Mystic No.	Question.	Oracles.	Mystic No.
1	Mars	V	31	Genii	XXXV
2	Pluto	IV	32	Lares	XXXIV
3	Neptune	III	33	Penates	XXXIII
4	Saturn	II	34	Centaurs	XXXII
5	Jupiter	I	35	Tritons	XXXI
6	Charon	LX	36	Satyrs	XXX
7	Rhadamanthus	LIX	37	Fauns	XXIX
8	Minos	LVIII	38	Nymphs	XXVIII
9	Prometheus	LVII	39	Muses	XXVII
10	Aristeus	LVI	40	Sibyls	XXVI
11	Æsculapius	LV	41	Feronia	XXV
12	Perseus	LIV	42	Latona	XXIV
13	Orpheus	LIII	43	Pomona	XXIII
14	Atlas	LII	44	Cybele	XXII
15	Achilles	LI	45	Flora	XXI
16	Hercules	L	46	Themis	XX
17	Theseus	XLIX	47	Minerva	XIX
18	Jason	XLVIII	48	Diana	XVIII
19	Janus	XLVII	49	Proserpine	XVII
20	Priapus	XLVI	50	Juno	XVI
21	Serapis	XLV	51	Bellona	XV
22	Momus	XLIV	52	Aurora	XIV
23	Æolus	XLIII	53	Venus	XIII
24	Cerberus	XLII	54	Ceres	XII
25	Furies	XLI	55	Vesta	XI
26	Lamiæ	XL	56	Mercury	X
27	Harpies	XXXIX	57	Apollo	IX
28	Syrens	XXXVIII	58	Pan	VIII
29	Giants	XXXVII	59	Vulcan	VII
30	Fates	XXXVI	60	Bacchus	VI

FORTUNA SEPTIMA

Question.	Oracles.	Mystic No.	Question.	Oracles.	Mystic No.
1	Bacchus	VI	31	Fates	XXXVI
2	Mars	V	32	Genii	XXXV
3	Pluto	IV	33	Lares	XXXIV
4	Neptune	III	34	Penates	XXXIII
5	Saturn	II	35	Centaurs	XXXII
6	Jupiter	I	36	Tritons	XXXI
7	Charon	LX	37	Satyrs	XXX
8	Rhadamanthus	LIX	38	Fauns	XXIX
9	Minos	LVIII	39	Nymphs	XXVIII
10	Prometheus	LVII	40	Muses	XXVII
11	Aristeus	LVI	41	Sibyls	XXVI
12	Æsculapius	LV	42	Feronia	XXV
13	Perseus	LIV	43	Latona	XXIV
14	Orpheus	LIII	44	Pomona	XXIII
15	Atlas	LII	45	Cybele	XXII
16	Achilles	LI	46	Flora	XXI
17	Hercules	L	47	Themis	XX
18	Theseus	XLIX	48	Minerva	XIX
19	Jason	XLVIII	49	Diana	XVIII
20	Janus	XLVII	50	Proserpine	XVII
21	Priapus	XLVI	51	Juno	XVI
22	Serapis	XLV	52	Bellona	XV
23	Momus	XLIV	53	Aurora	XIV
24	Æolus	XLIII	54	Venus	XIII
25	Cerberus	XLII	55	Ceres	XII
26	Furies	XLI	56	Vesta	XI
27	Lamiæ	XL	57	Mercury	X
28	Harpies	XXXIV	58	Apollo	IX
29	Syrens	XXXVIII	59	Pan	VIII
30	Giants	XXXVII	60	Vulcan	VII

FORTUNA OCTAVA

Question.	Oracles.	Mystic No.	Question.	Oracles.	Mystic No.
1	Vulcan	VII	31	Giants	XXXVII
2	Bacchus	VI	32	Fates	XXXVI
3	Mars	V	33	Genii	XXXV
4	Pluto	IV	34	Lares	XXXIV
5	Neptune	III	35	Penates	XXXIII
6	Saturn	II	36	Centaurs	XXXII
7	Jupiter	I	37	Tritons	XXXI
8	Charon	LX	38	Satyrs	XXX
9	Rhadamanthus	LIX	39	Fauns	XXIX
10	Minos	LVIII	40	Nymphs	XXVIII
11	Prometheus	LVII	41	Muses	XXVII
12	Aristeus	LVI	42	Sibyls	XXVI
13	Æsculapius	LV	43	Feronia	XXV
14	Perseus	LIV	44	Latona	XXIV
15	Orpheus	LIII	45	Pomona	XXIII
16	Atlas	LII	46	Cybele	XXII
17	Achilles	LI	47	Flora	XXI
18	Hercules	L	48	Themis	XX
19	Theseus	XLIX	49	Minerva	XIX
20	Jason	XLVIII	50	Diana	XVIII
21	Janus	XLVII	51	Proserpine	XVII
22	Priapus	XLVI	52	Juno	XVI
23	Serapis	XLV	53	Bellona	XV
24	Momus	XLIV	54	Aurora	XIV
25	Æolus	XLIII	55	Venus	XIII
26	Cerberus	XLII	56	Ceres	XII
27	Furies	XLI	57	Vesta	XI
28	Lamiæ	XL	58	Mercury	X
29	Harpies	XXXIX	59	Apollo	IX
30	Syrens	XXXVIII	60	Pan	VIII

FORTUNA NONA

Question.	Oracles.	Mystic No.	Question.	Oracles.	Mystic No.
1	Pan	VIII	31	Syrens	XXXVIII
2	Vulcan	VII	32	Giants	XXXVII
3	Bacchus	VI	33	Fates	XXXVI
4	Mars	V	34	Genii	XXXV
5	Pluto	IV	35	Lares	XXXIV
6	Neptune	III	36	Penates	XXXIII
7	Saturn	II	37	Centaurs	XXXII
8	Jupiter	I	38	Tritons	XXXI
9	Charon	LX	39	Satyrs	XXX
10	Rhadamanthus	LIX	40	Fauns	XXIX
11	Minos	LVIII	41	Nymphs	XXVIII
12	Prometheus	LVII	42	Muses	XXVII
13	Aristeus	LVI	43	Sibyls	XXVI
14	Æsculapius	LV	44	Feronia	XXV
15	Perseus	LIV	45	Latona	XXIV
16	Orpheus	LIII	46	Pomona	XXIII
17	Atlas	LII	47	Cybele	XXII
18	Achilles	LI	48	Flora	XXI
19	Hercules	L	49	Themis	XX
20	Theseus	XLIX	50	Minerva	XIX
21	Jason	XLVIII	51	Diana	XVIII
22	Janus	XLVII	52	Proserpine	XVII
23	Priapus	XLVI	53	Juno	XVI
24	Serapis	XLV	54	Bellona	XV
25	Momus	XLIV	55	Aurora	XIV
26	Æolus	XLIII	56	Venus	XIII
27	Cerberus	XLII	57	Ceres	XII
28	Furies	XLI	58	Vesta	XI
29	Lamiæ	XL	59	Mercury	X
30	Harpies	XXXIX	60	Apollo	IX

FORTUNA DECIMA

Question.	Oracles.	Mystic No.	Question.	Oracles.	Mystic No.
1	Apollo	IX	31	Harpies	XXXIX
2	Pan	VIII	32	Syrens	XXXVIII
3	Vulcan	VII	33	Giants	XXXVII
4	Bacchus	VI	34	Fates	XXXVI
5	Mars	V	35	Genii	XXXV
6	Pluto	IV	36	Lares	XXXIV
7	Neptune	III	37	Penates	XXXIII
8	Saturn	II	38	Centaurs	XXXII
9	Jupiter	I	39	Tritons	XXXI
10	Charon	LX	40	Satyrs	XXX
11	Rhadamanthus	LIX	41	Fauns	XXIX
12	Minos	LVIII	42	Nymphs	XXVIII
13	Prometheus	LVII	43	Muses	XXVII
14	Aristeus	LVI	44	Sibyls	XXVI
15	Æsculapius	LV	45	Feronia	XXV
16	Perseus	LIV	46	Latona	XXIV
17	Orpheus	LIII	47	Pomona	XXIII
18	Atlas	LII	48	Cybele	XXII
19	Achilles	LI	49	Flora	XXI
20	Hercules	L	50	Themis	XX
21	Theseus	XLIX	51	Minerva	XIX
22	Jason	XLVIII	52	Diana	XVIII
23	Janus	XLVII	53	Proserpine	XVII
24	Priapus	XLVI	54	Juno	XVI
25	Serapis	XLV	55	Bellona	XV
26	Momus	XLIV	56	Aurora	XIV
27	Æolus	XLIII	57	Venus	XIII
28	Cerberus	XLII	58	Ceres	XII
29	Furies	XLI	59	Vesta	XI
30	Lamiæ	XL	60	Mercury	X

FORTUNA UNDECIMA

Question.	Oracles.	Mystic No.	Question.	Oracles.	Mystic No.
1	Mercury	X	31	Lamiæ	XL
2	Apollo	IX	32	Harpies	XXXIX
3	Pan	VIII	33	Syrens	XXXVIII
4	Vulcan	VII	34	Giants	XXXVII
5	Bacchus	VI	35	Fates	XXXVI
6	Mars	V	36	Genii	XXXV
7	Pluto	IV	37	Lares	XXXIV
8	Neptune	III	38	Penates	XXXIII
9	Saturn	II	39	Centaurs	XXXII
10	Jupiter	I	40	Tritons	XXXI
11	Charon	LX	41	Satyrs	XXX
12	Rhadamanthus	LIX	42	Fauns	XXIX
13	Minos	LVIII	43	Nymphs	XXVIII
14	Prometheus	LVII	44	Muses	XXVII
15	Aristeus	LVI	45	Sibyls	XXVI
16	Æsculapius	LV	46	Feronia	XXV
17	Perseus	LIV	47	Latona	XXIV
18	Orpheus	LIII	48	Pomona	XXIII
19	Atlas	LII	49	Cybele	XXII
20	Achilles	LI	50	Flora	XXI
21	Hercules	L	51	Themis	XX
22	Theseus	XLIX	52	Minerva	XIX
23	Jason	XLVIII	53	Diana	XVIII
24	Janus	XLVII	54	Proserpine	XVII
25	Priapus	XLVI	55	Juno	XVI
26	Serapis	XLV	56	Bellona	XV
27	Momus	XLIV	57	Aurora	XIV
28	Æolus	XLIII	58	Venus	XIII
29	Cerberus	XLII	59	Ceres	XII
30	Furies	XLI	60	Vesta	XI

FORTUNA DUODECIMA

Question.	Oracles.	Mystic No.	Question.	Oracles.	Mystic No.
1	Vesta	XI	31	Furies	XLI
2	Mercury	X	32	Lamiæ	XL
3	Apollo	IX	33	Harpies	XXXIX
4	Pan	VIII	34	Syrens	XXXVIII
5	Vulcan	VII	35	Giants	XXXVII
6	Bacchus	VI	36	Fates	XXXVI
7	Mars	V	37	Genii	XXXV
8	Pluto	IV	38	Lares	XXXIV
9	Neptune	III	39	Penates	XXXIII
10	Saturn	II	40	Centaurs	XXXII
11	Jupiter	I	41	Tritons	XXXI
12	Charon	LX	42	Satyrs	XXX
13	Rhadamanthus	LIX	43	Fauns	XXIX
14	Minos	LVIII	44	Nymphs	XXVIII
15	Prometheus	LVII	45	Muses	XXVII
16	Aristeus	LVI	46	Sibyls	XXVI
17	Æsculapius	LV	47	Feronia	XXV
18	Perseus	LIV	48	Latona	XXIV
19	Orpheus	LIII	49	Pomona	XXIII
20	Atlas	LII	50	Cybele	XXII
21	Achilles	LI	51	Flora	XXI
22	Hercules	L	52	Themis	XX
23	Theseus	XLIX	53	Minerva	XIX
24	Jason	XLVIII	54	Diana	XVIII
25	Janus	XLVII	55	Proserpine	XVII
26	Priapus	XLVI	56	Juno	XVI
27	Serapis	XLV	57	Bellona	XV
28	Momus	XLIV	58	Aurora	XIV
29	Æolus	XLIII	59	Venus	XIII
30	Cerberus	XLII	60	Ceres	XII

THE ANSWERS OF THE GODS

I.—Jupiter

Jupiter, the God of men and King of all the gods, son of Saturn and of Rhea, utters the oracles and confers the marks and seals of glory and ambition.

1. He has at present, but ambition will strip him.
2. He will be the fortune of his parents.
3. His life will be long and happy.
4. He will be fortunate in marriage.
5. This is a very good subject ; he will be received favourably.
6. He will be one day at the top of his profession.
7. He will persevere in the calling adopted and will always live in contentment.
8. You cannot fail to be happy.
9. You will not remain therein, but will be advanced by influential people.
10. Take time by the forelock and profit by the present good auspices.
11. Your friends are of very good position, and she will therefore succeed.
12. They will be good managers, honest and endowed with foresight.

II.—Saturn

The son of heaven and of Vesta is the God of Time and promises nothing but happiness.

1. You will die in your native land.
2. He is too mistrustful of himself to have lost it.
3. Felicity will accompany him everywhere.
4. His will be a long life and he will survive all his brothers.
5. Marriage will promote your welfare.
6. He will long enjoy this reversion.
7. He will be intriguing and will make many friends.
8. He will die in harness and also in the odour of sanctity.
9. Your length of days will insure you the most advantageous occupations.
10. Remain under him; he entertains a certain regard for you.
11. Go on; you are doing well.
12. She will be happy.

III.—Neptune

Issue of the Time-God Saturn and of Ops, Neptune was set over the sea and all waters; his oracles are those of inconstancy and adventure.

1. You would die in poverty, were it not for an inheritance which will come to you some time prior to your death.
2. There are those who believe that he has it, but they are mistaken.
3. You will fall among thieves by water and when you die, you will be still in their toils.
4. His life will be chequered but his later days happy.
5. He will die when it will be thought that he is in the best of health.
6. He will marry, and after the death of his better half he is likely to go into the church.
7. It will be carried by the majority to his advantage.
8. He must be sent to America.
9. He will first go into the church and later on into the army.
10. He will take advantage of your natural simplicity to play you a nasty trick.
11. They regard you as rough and awkward, but they do you a wrong therein.
12. Be less retiring and more sociable.

IV.—Pluto

Son of Saturn and Rhea, Pluto was God of the Infernal Regions; his prognostications are ominous and even deadly.

1. You will die of apoplexy and be found in your bed.
2. You are likely to perish in a prison, but it will not be on a criminal charge.
3. A journey into remote countries will deprive you of the consolation of dying in your native land.
4. He has lost one half of it.
5. He will be unfortunate in his undertakings.
6. Be careful, or he will be suffocated by his nurse.
7. He will marry, and marriage will lead to his death.
8. He is arrested in mental development and will not be received.
9. Blunderers and wastrels will equal him.
10. His parents have forced him to take up with his present calling, and he is going to destruction therein.
11. You see too far in business, and he will detest you.
12. Be at ease; no one will dream of advancing you.

V.—Mars

All his oracles are those of blood, but glory is ever therein, for conquering Mars, son of Juno and a miraculous flower, is the God of War.

1. His time for death is not yet; he has still more to achieve, and he will therefore be restored.
2. He will die in the bed of honour.
3. You will die covered with glory and wealth.
4. You will die in the heat of action.
5. He has lost it through a pair of bright eyes.
6. He will be a great soldier and will die young in the army.
7. Born for war, his life will be a long victory.
8. The blood in your veins should lead you to a brilliant marriage.
9. He will be welcomed because of his father's bravery.
10. He will serve the State and will be loved for his great talent.
11. He is undoubtedly called thereto and will pass the rest of his life therein.
12. Manage him, and he will answer your purpose.

VI.—Bacchus

Son of Jupiter and Semele, and Deity of Wine, all Oracles of Bacchus deal with a medley of intoxication and wit.

1. His is a thirsty soul and he is often drawn thereto.
2. The disease is dangerous and the issue doubtful ; for him alcohol means death.
3. Wine is too heating for you ; be careful —you might die of pleurisy.
4. Persons of your type may look to die in want after wasting their substance in taverns.
5. You may die in the midst of a banquet.
6. He has at present, but he stands to lose it through excess.
7. The excesses of his youth will make him wise in old age.
8. If the nurse drinks wine, he will not die in his cradle.
9. A wife is a hindrance to drinking ; he will not marry.
10. His jowl is too red to get him such an appointment.
11. His bottle is dearer than his trade.
12. Wine will prove the loss of his position.

VII.—Vulcan

Son of Jupiter and Juno, Vulcan was smith of the gods; be careful, for his grime may soil you.

1. Expect no help at his hands.
2. He has produced only four sorts to-day.
3. A change of doctor is needed, or you will scarcely recover.
4. Your death, when it comes, will be sudden.
5. You will die, like a pilgrim of old, in stable or ditch, but it means that place matters nothing because your heart will be turned towards heaven.
6. You will die smoking.
7. He is safe, having nothing further to lose.
8. His hopes will be fair and high, but they will not bring him to prosperity.
9. The foolish love of the mother will prove the child's ruin.
10. He will marry a flirt, who will lead him a fine dance.
11. He is too frivolous and changeable to be tolerated.
12. He will have no special capacity for any kind of public service.

VIII.—Pan

Son of Mercury and Penelope, Pan was a rural deity, and he offers in his Oracles nothing but joy and content.

1. Your suspicion has fallen on the right person ; he is the thief whom you seek.

2. Take care ; he will scale the walls of the house to obtain an entrance.

3. He has certainly been there, but for jollity rather than drinking.

4. The care by which he is surrounded will draw him from the evil path.

5. You will die in your bed, and in a natural, painless manner.

6. If you wish to die rich, work in the days of your youth and be frugal.

7. You will pass out of this life in the arms of those who love you.

8. There is not much left for him to lose.

9. The peace of the country will charm him from his wild ways.

10. The child will live long, if the mother nurses him cheerfully.

11. He will not go into the church and he will not marry.

12. He has no particular talents, but his good spirits will make him welcome.

IX.—Apollo

Son of Jupiter and Latona, Apollo—the light of the world—was God of Music, of Medicine and Oracles. Erudite minds and people of genius should therefore find in his company the feast of reason and the flow of soul.

1. Trust her not; she will betray your secret.
2. The thief will come and confess to you of his own accord.
3. He will he himself the happiness of the house.
4. He does not frequent taverns; all excess is opposed to his studious turn.
5. There is no need for anxiety; he will return in health.
6. You will die in the odour of sanctity.
7. You will neither be rich nor poor towards the end of your life.
8. You will die amidst men of learning.
9. He is wise and without reproach.
10. Aptitude for the sciences will give him a good disposition.
11. His learning will make his demise regretted by many.
12. You are so studious that your life might well become like that of the cloister.

X.—Mercury

Son of Jupiter and of Maia, who was herself the daughter of Atlas, Mercury is the God of Eloquence, but the honours which he offers are fleeting.

1. That which you have lost is in the hands of one to whom you would have given it gladly.
2. She is secret and may be trusted entirely.
3. That which has been stolen will be restored, but you will never know the thief.
4. You will be perfectly satisfied with his services.
5. He would go there gladly but is hindered by questions of good taste, decorum or convention.
6. He is likely to die suddenly, as the result of a mistaken operation.
7. As your death will not be that of one who is illustrious, either for genius or learning, so strive that it may be a death of the just.
8. You will die happily.
9. You will die in the country, at the house of a friend.
10. He is seeking an opportunity to lose it utterly.
11. His eloquence of speech will commend him to those in power.
12. He will live long, enjoying the esteem of every one.

XI.—Vesta

The Oracles of this Goddess are elevated, for the daughter of Saturn and of Rhea is the Guardian of Fire.

1. Your dream seems to promise too much; you will be happy if half of it is fulfilled.
2. That which you have lost is not very far away.
3. If you trust your secret to her, she will disclose it inadvertently.
4. Those whom you suspect are innocent.
5. He will be more master than the master himself.
6. He has not been there to-day, but he was yesterday.
7. He will recover from all ills.
8. Your death will take place through neglect of remedies in the first stages of illness.
9. You will leave to your heirs a considerable substance which you will not have enjoyed long on your own part.
10. You will die between heaven and earth, but this oracle may have two meanings.
11. Do you, who ask, yourself possess this? Why expect that I have it?
12. He will gain honours by intrigues.

XII.—Ceres

She who is Goddess of Harvests, fair daughter of Saturn and of Rhea, will confer nothing but abundance.

1. You will win the action but not without heavy expense.
2. The dream foretells a great happiness to come.
3. You will find what you seek when it is least in your mind.
4. It is all one whether the secret is cried on the house-tops or told to the person in question.
5. He is a sharper, as you will discover shortly.
6. He will serve you faithfully.
7. Where could they deposit the required quantity ? He would empty the cellars.
8. He will return convalescent shortly.
9. You will die of exhaustion after considerable suffering.
10. You will certainly die very rich ; but how will it help you ?
11. There is some fear of a violent or sudden death in the midst of all plenty.
12. You will be alone in the world.

XIII.—Venus

Daughter of Jupiter and Diana, Venus is the Goddess of Love and she brings pleasures to many.

1. You will make a gain at play, but one greater through Cupid.
2. You will win your lawsuit, and you will be ruined.
3. An object beheld yesterday has put this phantom in your imagination.
4. The one whom you love most in the house where your loss occurred is the one who has found what you seek.
5. This person is as secret as a peal of thunder.
6. It will be more disastrous for you to know than to remain in ignorance.
7. Do not trust him with your daughters and then you will be quite content.
8. He goes to please his damsel.
9. He will be cured in appearance but will die in a short time, after a relapse.
10. A relapse will cause your death.
11. You have played long enough; do not regret the past; forget if possible, and do better in the future.
12. The cause of your death will be a debt owing to Nature—meaning, old age.

XIV.—Aurora

The way of fortune may be prepared by Aurora, daughter of Hyperion and Thea ; she is the herald of the Sun in its rising.

1. All days will be indifferent to you.
2. Be careful of speculation and gambling, if you would know happiness.
3. Give up the action at once ; you cannot win.
4. The great desire which you have for the thing dreamed of will make your dream come true.
5. You will obtain compensation for your loss from another source.
6. This is a good friend, in whom you may confide your secret.
7. Your friends are responsible for this evil.
8. He is entertaining, but he is ruining himself.
9. He is wary and circumspect ; his drinking is done at home, not at the tavern.
10. He will not die of this complaint.
11. An unfortunate accident will overtake you.
12. You will die blessed—rich in possessions and faithful children.

XV.—Bellona

Means for the satiation of the passions may be offered by the vindictive Bellona, who is the sister of Mars, and as he is the God so she is Goddess of War. But she gives nothing for nothing.

1. He is seeking a pretext to leave you.

2. One half of the week will favour your designs.

3. There are two games of chance in which you will win money, but you will be miserable notwithstanding.

4. The gifts which you bring will enable you to gain your end.

5. The dream warns you to take care of yourself.

6. That which you have lost is in the hands of thieves.

7. A present will open the lips of the one who knows your secret.

8. Suspect him who claims the chief part therein.

9. He is abusing your good nature.

10. Only too often.

11. Too many medicines are likely to send his soul on the great journey.

12. That which may cause your death is profound sadness and weariness.

XVI.—Juno

Daughter of Saturn and Rhea, Juno is Goddess of Riches, and if you are eager for these, she may help you.

1. He is well, he is rich; indeed he is very rich and the chief person in his district.
2. You will see him shortly, and he will bring you a present.
3. A substantial advantage should be yours on Sunday.
4. It will be a matter of surprise if you are fortunate at games of chance.
5. You must win over those who can influence the chief person concerned in this business.
6. The dream foretells a great happiness to come.
7. You will recover what you have lost in time.
8. It is impossible to be more secret.
9. You will learn something from a neighbour.
10. Be regular in your payments to him, and he will serve you well.
11. The tavern makes beggars, but he is rich.
12. If only the evil were known, it would soon be cured.

XVII.—Proserpine

Goddess of the Infernal Regions, daughter of Jupiter and Ceres, the oracles of Proserpine are oracles of womanhood.

1. Modesty forbids her to undertake the journey alone; she awaits company.
2. She is in a place where her beauty will lose none of its charm.
3. She is thinking of her grief at parting from you and going by herself.
4. Feasts, merrymakings and public holidays are not without danger for you.
5. Avoid games of chance; you will lose.
6. Justice and equity are not in your favour.
7. Your hope is a dream only.
8. Abstain from consulting palmists, astrologers and tellers of fortune; you may hear more than you wish.
9. The person is secret, but you cannot hide from yourself.
10. Look among those in the house; it is the one whom you would think of last.
11. Do not be intimate with him; he is a trickster and will overreach you.
12. He goes seldom and not then by himself.

XVIII.—Diana

Daughter of Jupiter and Latona, Goddess of the Chase, Diana prophesies concerning things of the lesser fortunes.

1. You may do something at sport and more in boon companionship, to your own detriment. Mars does not need a soldier of your sort.
2. He is delayed by many welcomes and much good cheer.
3. He is living in clover and cares for nothing.
4. He is talking of you and drinking your health.
5. Monday will be fortunate for your stomach.
6. Never play for money.
7. Take care of your lawyer and he will take care of your case.
8. The dream is an aftermath of the supper, for this went before it.
9. You may have news between courses at dinner.
10. She will keep the secret till evening, but it will come out subsequently.
11. The thief is a fat man, and this is all that you will ever learn about him.
12. You can trust him with everything, except the key of the wine-cellar.

XIX.—Minerva

This is the Goddess of Wisdom, who sprang in the perfection of her form from the brain of Jupiter, shining with arts and sciences. She presides—in prophetic things—over questions of scholarship, learning and genius.

1. You will attain success in some great city, but if you dwell already in one, you may have to go further.

2. You will perform acts of valour or military skill which will cause admiration not only in your immediate superior officers but in the generals and field-marshal.

3. The fame and consideration which are his in the place where he is now staying will not permit of his speedy return.

4. He is well, and better than you; he is becoming an able man, while you have everything to learn and do.

5. He is asleep and dreaming pleasantly of you.

6. Attempt nothing on a Saturday; that day is unlucky for your chances.

7. You will always be unlucky at gambling, but you will succeed in study.

8. Your elegance of speech will make an impression everywhere, and you will gain infallibly.

9. You are sensible enough not to trouble about this dream.

10. Forget her; she is at her own amusements; you will never regain her.

11. Confide in him as much as you like; he is quite safe; on account of his preoccupations he will not even know what you say.

12. One who claims to be your best friend is playing off this trick upon you.

XX.—Themis

This daughter of Heaven and Earth is the adorable Goddess of Justice; consult her on things that are just and her answers will be true.

1. Prosecute the proposed enterprise; there is much to gain.
2. Where you are least known you will succeed best.
3. Avoid military affairs; they mean loss of life.
4. There may be a quicker return than you will want.
5. He has died bravely.
6. He thinks that you have forgotten him.
7. Let Wednesday be counted among your unfavourable days.
8. If you stake your last farthing, you will lose it.

9. Without better evidence, you stand to lose the case.

10. Laugh at a dream like this; it is mere folly.

11. You will have to buy back what you have lost, if you wish to have it.

12. He will not only tell your secret but make it worse by embellishments.

XXI.—Flora

The Goddess of Flowers and Bride of Zephyr speaks only of fleeting things.

1. A good inheritance awaits you, but you will not enjoy it long.

2. Withdraw from the business; you will lose therein.

3. If you cannot make a fortune in your own country, do not expect it elsewhere.

4. You will die in action, but in the forefront, on a bed of honour.

5. He will return shortly in a sad plight.

6. Pray God for him; he is in great affliction.

7. He is in trouble and there is no consolation in his cross.

8. Do not conclude any business on a Tuesday.

9. Be content with a single winning; to do more is to risk loss.

10. However good your cause may be, you will lose it.

11. Your dream will only be fulfilled by chance.

12. What profits it to recover that which you will only lose again, and this time for good and all ?

XXII.—Cybele

Daughter of Heaven and of Vesta, Goddess of the Earth, Cybele was wife of Saturn, and she gives strength in adversity.

1. Expect more from strangers than from your relatives.

2. Your relations are not in a position to bequeath you anything.

3. If you are forced into bankruptcy, you will involve others therein.

4. Your good behaviour will make you happy.

5. You will be killed in the first action or live long in arms.

6. Illness will detain him where he is for another month.

7. His death would dishonour his relations, if they knew of it.

8. He has entirely forgotten you.

9. All times and seasons will be ill-starred in your case.

10. Men of consideration and honour shun the gamester.

11. You will lose your case through a false witness.

12. The dream is a pure illusion.

XXIII.—Pomona

Goddess of Fruits and wife of Vertumnus, the God of Gardens, Pomona is a giver of good appearances and good positions.

1. You will have no better chance of attaining happiness than during this present year.

2. From your friends, if you can manage them properly.

3. There are some who may help you to an eminent position.

4. You will become rich and powerful, owing to this business.

5. There is something to be said for the southern parts of Europe.

6. You will rise to an office of importance.

7. He is on the way and impatient to see you.

8. He is doing himself well where you sent him and will not return too soon.

9. He is planning to come back to see you.

10. Alternate days in the week will be good for you.

11. It is possible in your case that speculations will be your chance of profit.

12. You will gain your suit in rather an underhand way.

XXIV.—Latona

She was daughter of Cœus, the Titan, and Phœbe: her rule is over things connected with envy.

1. She cannot forego marriage.

2. Envy and ill-speaking will there work against you.

3. Expect nothing from anyone, seeing that you are universally detested.

4. Your inheritance will prove ruinous through lawsuits.

5. A merchant on whom you rely will do you a great wrong.

6. Avoid the envious, and where you are free from these you will do well.

7. Your courage will rescue a person in high place from a great danger; you will have your reward; but afterwards you will be undone by jealousy.

8. He does not wish to return, but the envious compel him to do so sooner than he intends.

9. You would be sorry to know the truth about the life he is leading.

10. There are those who would make him break with you, but he loves you too much to leave you.

11. Your origin is a matter of envy with some of your kidney.

12. You are one who is sure to be fleeced at gambling.

XXV.—Feronia

The Goddess of Woods and Forests will show you how to avoid evil occasions.

1. Do not chatter and cajole; peace will then reign in the house.

2. He prefers to be alone, rather than to have an ill-assorted companion.

3. You are liable to have a fall in that place, and the consequence will be a dangerous illness.

4. It depends on your good conduct, and this should rule your actions.

5. Do not encourage the sentiment; she would harm you.

6. The bad faith of your associate will ruin you, unless you are careful.

7. Change both your inclination and your place; your fortune will then be assured.

8. Do not enter the army; it is likely to cost you your life.

9. Return is hindered by difficulties in travelling.

10. You will soon have news, and if he rejects your advice, he will presently change his views.

11. She is planning to annoy you.

12. Avoid unfortunate occasions and happiness will be always yours.

XXVI.—Sibyls

These were virgin soothsayers and advisers of the Gods ; expect good oracles from them.

1. The husband will die first and the wife shortly after.

2. The troubles are the husband's indifference and the money wasted on his pleasures.

3. She is now her own mistress and will give way no longer.

4. It will bring you great content.

5. A faithful servant will be your way to fortune.

6. You have no inheritance to look for.

7. Be faithful in your accounts and you will not be put to the blush.

8. You will be better off by sea than by land.

9. The poultry-farm is more in your line than the battle-field.

10. You will soon see him restored to perfect health.

11. He is alive and well.

12. Her thoughts are as your thoughts.

XXVII.—Muses

Cherish these Divine Sisters, O lovers of science: their oracles are those of immortal fame.

1. She is with child of a boy, who will become a poet.
2. The wife will die first, and it will be almost through joy.
3. Domestic disorder results from the wife's luxury and the universal praise of her abilities.
4. Her love of literature is like to make her a recluse rather than one who remarries.
5. You will make a friend who will bring you great happiness and indeed lasting fame.
6. Of God alone, Who is the sole and only good.
7. You will have one that is eternal.
8. Follow your own bent, and your business will make you famous.
9. You will be illustrious in study.
10. Your bent is towards learned research rather than a soldier's life.

11. Let him finish the work he has undertaken and he will return famous.

12. He will come back weary but covered with glory.

XXVIII.—Nymphs

Daughters of Nereus and Doris, these Deities of the Water will make you pleasant prognostications.

1. Their children will be beautiful.

2. Handsome twins will be born to them.

3. They will die on the same day and be buried together.

4. There would be more domestic happiness if the wife had a little more taste for amusements.

5. She is young and beautiful; she does not wish to pass her best days in sadness.

6. You will be elevated to a degree of honour which you have not expected.

7. An unknown person will be your fortune.

8. Pay attention to the good old lady, and you will benefit by her.

9. A voyage to the East would increase your business.

10. A journey through one of the Latin countries will prove to your advantage.

11. You will die owing to a false alarm.

12. Let him open his eyes and see how he has been duped: it will bring him speedily to his senses.

XXIX.—Fauns

These are the brood of Faunus, the rural Deity, and they utter oracles only on evil things.

1. You will not marry, in case worse should befall you.
2. Sterility in this instance is the consequence of evil life on both sides.
3. Her husband's ill treatment may cause a miscarriage.
4. The wife will occasion her husband's death a year after their marriage, but these things occur sometimes through fatal mischance.
5. They do not get on together because they have never loved one another.
6. The first husband's bad temper makes the idea of another marriage repulsive.
7. You will lose the good opinion of those who now esteem you.
8. You will be always more or less necessitous, so expect no permanent help from anyone.
9. Of what use would you find an inheritance, seeing that you squander everything?

10. Have nothing to do with the business; it is dishonourable and must do you harm.

11. In dissipation and gambling.

12. Your baseness is likely to bring you to a bad end.

XXX.—Satyrs

These are woodland Gods, and their presages are mostly evil.

1. Your wife troubles herself very little about you.

2. You are likely to regret the only marriage which you are likely to make.

3. They will have no children.

4. She will have one daughter and will spoil her.

5. The length of their companionship will become wearisome to both.

6. The cause of trouble is the wife's flirtations, which are intolerable to the husband.

7. She is quite willing to remarry, but no one comes forward.

8. She will be your fatality in all things.

9. What seek you? Idleness and ignorance are your lot.

10. The death of your wife would bring you a heritage of woe.

11. Seek no more than is needful for your easy maintenance.

12. There is no permanence in sight, wherever you settle.

XXXI.—Tritons

These are Sea-Gods, and they deal in loud alarms.

1. Your husband will be a good man and will let you do as you please without interference.
2. Promptitude will be her chief characteristic.
3. You will only have one wife, but she will have several husbands.
4. The answer is that they will, but it would be better for them were it otherwise.
5. She will hurt herself before she has done.
6. Their happiness will be short-lived, and the wife will be first to die.
7. The barrenness of the one disappoints the other.
8. She may survive several husbands.
9. While there, you will be almost continually ill.
10. A large fortune will be left you by a relative who has manifested little affection so far.
11. You will only have that which you manage to make for yourself.
12. Your business will grow steadily.

XXXII.—Centaurs

These were children of Centaurus and Stilbia, creatures of monstrous fame, and that which they foretell may be usually taken in the opposite sense of the words.

1. The parties are on bad terms, and this is likely to ruin the family.
2. He will be a journeyman, and his humour will vary with his work.
3. She will be cross and peevish till you let her do as she likes.
4. You will be long a widower and will be approaching seventy before you marry again.
5. They will have three daughters and a boy.
6. There is likelihood of a still-born child only, or one which will live but few hours or days.
7. The wife will be first to pass into the next world and will reserve a place for her husband.
8. The intolerable arrogance of the one will not be agreeable to the other.
9. She will not remarry, but will lead a life of devotion.
10. You will suffer much therein.
11. It means fortune, if you can manage her.
12. The answer is yes, if one whom you know of should die.

XXXIII.—Penates

These are Household Gods, sons of Mercury and Lara: their's are oracles of consolation.

1. Follow up the matter, or the ground will be cut from under your feet.
2. Never was marriage more fortunate.
3. He will love you sincerely, and you will find happiness with him.
4. You will be loved devotedly by your wife.
5. You will enter once only into the wedded state, and you will have every satisfaction therein.
6. They will have children in whom they will find all that they desire.
7. She will be delivered of a son safely.
8. The pair will in no sense regret this present life and will indeed quit it joyfully in succession.
9. The bad dispositions of the children dislocate the marriage bond.
10. She will remarry to please her parents.
11. Many tears and then honours thereafter—these await you.
12. An unexpected inheritance will enrich you.

XXXIV.—Lares

These twin-Gods are of the same parentage as the Penates; they are the tutelary Deities of towns, and they teach worldly wisdom.

1. Endeavour to win the parents, and you will obtain that which you desire.
2. Manage her mother, and she will grant your wish.
3. The wife's obedience will maintain peace.
4. He will be prompt, and unless you are yielding you may feel the consequences.
5. I answer for his fidelity, but not for its permanence.
6. You will not marry again, being satisfied with the position which you have gained.
7. You will have children; train them well, and they will make your fortune.
8. She will have a daughter of great beauty and like herself in disposition.
9. Do not seek this; it may give offence to your spouse, who will die first.
10. Debts consume the house and are causing the separation: be satisfied with a little.
11. Her love for the children will prevent her marrying again.
12. Trust no one; do not say what you think; and you will be quite successful.

XXXV.—Genii

Sons of Jupiter and Earth, these daimons are both good and bad: sometimes their oracles rejoice and sometimes sadden.

1. Your marriage will bring you many joys and more than many regrets.
2. She will care for you more than her parents will do, the latter having no wish for the alliance.
3. They will have difficulty in persuading her to wed you.
4. Your wife may have cause to regret her freedom.
5. Your husband will be a miser, who will stint you in bare necessaries.
6. She will want to be mistress and have everything pass through her hands.
7. You will marry twice, against your own will.
8. They will have children who will ruin them.
9. She will have a seven-month child—a boy.
10. The husband will die first, through grief at the loss of the child whom he loves most.
11. It is you who are too much in love to play the fool.
12. Affection for the deceased prevents her from entertaining a second marriage; but time may change this.

XXXVI.—Fates

These are holders of Destiny and these can instruct therein; they are daughters of Jupiter and Themis.

1. He has sense and wit, but his disposition is gloomy and double-faced.
2. You will be married, but your happiness will be short-lived.
3. Your hopes are vain; you will never marry her.
4. Do not trust her; she has promised another, whom she loves devotedly.
5. The want of children may lead to divorce.
6. Drink will be your husband's only love.
7. She will be outwardly most devoted, but it is a devotion for which you will smart.
8. You will wed only one woman.
9. They will have many boys.
10. The wife will give birth to a daughter.
11. An ill-starred voyage will separate them soon after their honeymoon.
12. The wife's intolerable disposition leads to this separation.

XXXVII.—Giants

These are children of Earth and being incarnations of pride their oracles are those of humiliation.

1. You have no friends because you are incapable of friendship.
2. He has a modicum of talent but is violent and headstrong.
3. You will not marry so quickly; there will be questions of worldly estate, and there may be other questions.
4. Marriage will not be to your profit.
5. Your good looks are scarcely sufficient to make her accept you.
6. You will have plenty of time to repent, for the ways of your wife will humble you.
7. He is a master of cajolery; his chief ambition is also to have a good time.
8. She will always be chiding, and you will have no peace with her.
9. Your first wife will kill all wish for another.
10. The woman is barren ground.
11. Her child will be a daughter.
12. She will die at the birth of her first child.

XXXVIII.—Syrens

They were daughters of Achelous and Melpomene; their oracles are brazen, like their ways.

1. Your thoughts are impertinent and foolish: cease to cherish them.
2. Your friends are faithful to you, which is more than you can say.
3. His is the art of pleasing and ingratiating himself with the innocent; but he is a man of pleasure.
4. Unless you marry within six months, you will not do so for ten years.
5. A rival will spoil your plans.
6. Make much of her, and you will win.
7. So much effrontery and boldness will destroy your peace and thwart you always.
8. He will love gambling and drinking.
9. Your wife will be addicted to cards and flirtation.
10. You will marry three wives, two of whom will be widows.
11. Be more steady, and then you may have what you wish.
12. The indications are in favour of a boy.

XXXIX.—Harpies

These monsters were born of Neptune and the Earth ; they deal in rapine and excess.

1. Flattery and baseness are the best way to secure her.

2. Your robberies will bring about the opposite of what you expect.

3. Your vexatious and libertine disposition can secure you no friend.

4. He presumes much upon himself, but he is honest and he pleases women.

5. You will marry before long, but much to the surprise of many.

6. You have posed and procrastinated too much, and the marriage will not take place.

7. You will win her, but she will not be pleased with your oddities.

8. The marriage will bring you joys innumerable, but they will not last ; sooner or later you will find yourself like a moth at a candle.

9. Your husband will love meetings, debates and even legal embroilments : you will not see much of him at home.

10. She will like to have elbow-room.

11. You will only deserve one, but you will have two.

12. Be less inconstant : do as you should by her, and she will do well by you.

XL.—Lamiæ

These are sorceresses and workers of evil charms: beware of such.

1. It is true and if it has not come about, it will still take place as said.
2. You will be indebted for your life and honour to their affection.
3. You possess already one half of what you desire.
4. You have only one friend whom you can trust.
5. He is small of mind and mean of spirit.
6. You will marry soon but not without reproaches.
7. Those whom you deem faithful will betray you over this marriage.
8. A master-stroke is needed for you to secure her.
9. The wife's caprices will occasion plenty of gossip.
10. Your husband will be kind and upright, but he will not be the husband for you.
11. Take care: his tastes are those of the playhouse and music-hall.
12. The happiness of your first marriage will make you think twice about a second one.

XLI.—Furies

These are daughters of Acheron and of Night; they exercise the judgment of Tartarus, and their counsel may undo you.

1. You will have a benefice but will lose it by lapse of right.
2. Those who declare it is so, and that it ought to happen, are really thinking the opposite; notwithstanding, happen it will.
3. It would be better far if you had never known them.
4. When you are wiser, what is now in your thoughts will be accomplished.
5. Pick out your true friends, for many are betraying you.
6. He is too ambitious and too fond of speculation.
7. You will meet with so many obstacles that you will abandon the marriage.
8. You will never obtain the lady if she will not make a confidant of her mother.
9. You will do well to give her up; the marriage is not advantageous, and you know why.
10. They will squander all that they possess.
11. Your husband will love good cheer and will be indifferent as to how it is obtained.
12. She will shew you what you could dispense with seeing.

XLII.—Cerberus

The dog of Pluto, born of Typhon and Echidne, is sometimes a friend at need.

1. Beware of this person.
2. When you are properly qualified, you will have a good appointment.
3. Do not trust the news: there is no foundation.
4. You expect love from these people, but they will only bring you to confusion.
5. You must check-mate the secret moves of an enemy, to reach the object of your plan.
6. Trust no one: those whom you regard as friends are anything but friends to you.
7. He has no malice: he wishes well to all.
8. In six months' time you will marry a beautiful girl—for love on both sides—and a happy life to follow.
9. There are great difficulties regarding this marriage.
10. You will have your desire: she wishes it as much as you do.
11. Your marriage is based on intrigue and cannot be happy.
12. Your husband will be your honour and your glory.

XLIII.—Æolus

The son of Hippotas rules the wind and can teach you to rule your passions.

1. Do not entertain the proposal; it will bring you no good.
2. A false report has bred enmity against you.
3. Your disadvantages will hinder church preferment.
4. The fact that they affirm it offers some evidence that it is not so.
5. Their benevolence will involve you in many oppositions.
6. Be patient, and your plan will succeed.
7. None of your friends are unfaithful, O doubting heart!
8. Let him live in clover, give him his full fling, and it will be possible to keep on with him.
9. You will be married against your will in a year's time.
10. Do not hurry; temporise, act prudently, and all will go well.
11. Keep within bounds; you will win her after much pursuit.
12. It should be so, but guard against changes and do your duty.

XLIV.—Momus

The Son of Sleep and of Night may amuse himself at your expense: read his oracles with judgment.

1. You are about to meet with a good turn of fortune.
2. Do not commit yourself: they are seeking to embarrass you.
3. Seem to fall in with his wishes, for the sake of peace.
4. If you reach forty years without attaining a competence, you need expect none.
5. The report has been spread to amuse a great many people.
6. You will displease them in a few months' time as much as you please them now.
7. Do not cherish such a thought; this will not come to pass.
8. Faithful or not, what do you care?
9. He is not over prudent, but he is a jovial fellow.
10. Speed the marriage, or you stand to lose your mistress.
11. Gain the parents, and that which you want will follow.
12. You are losing time and labour; you will not attain your wishes.

XLV.—Serapis

Serapis was adored by the Egyptians under the symbol of a Bull, and his oracles tend to obscurity.

1. You are feeding on foolish imaginations: cease to dwell thereon.
2. You have no ambition, but you are not devoid of vices.
3. Direct your thoughts elsewhere; in this quarter you will come to no good.
4. He does not care to see you face to face.
5. You will get some church preferment, but the question is how or why.
6. Those who propagate the rumour do so of set purpose.
7. If you do not share their feelings, you will lose their goodwill.
8. The envious will mar your plans.
9. Those who would have friends must win them. Can you do so?
10. He is not bad at heart, whatever he may seem outwardly.
11. You will never marry: who would share your lot? It may yet be great.
12. The marriage will take place: it will be a case of two fools together; but you will both remain content.

XLVI.—Priapus

This is the son of Venus and of Bacchus, who deals only in excesses.

1. You are likely to be glutted with excesses, and this is the path to the gutter.
2. Your desires are evil, and you will not bring them to pass.
3. You have some, but it is to make them minister to your pleasures.
4. Give less time to enjoyment, and think more of her.
5. He pretends to be reconciled with you and it is really his great wish.
6. Those of disorderly life are unfitted for high posts.
7. I believe it thoroughly, and I believe even more.
8. You will lose their good will by your conduct.
9. That which you have in your mind will come to pass only with difficulty: be, however, circumspect.
10. Friends of your stamp are not very faithful.
11. He is too fond of trifling.
12. You are far too fickle and will scarcely find a partner.

XLVII.—Janus

This was a King of Italy and a prince of prudence.

1. Do not expect to better your condition by changing it.
2. You will not die in business-harness ; you will have retired a few years.
3. You will attain that which you desire in a little time.
4. You will care nothing for appointments, but will like being chosen.
5. This business will turn out to your advantage.
6. Get your friends to intervene, or he will do you a bad turn.
7. Your prudence and zeal will compel your principals to advance you.
8. Watch those who have an interest in the matter, and the truth about it will be the reverse of anything they say.
9. Be of good heart ; they love and will love you always.
10. Tell your plan to no one, and you will succeed.
11. You would have many friends if you knew how to spare them ; exercise greater prudence.
12. He is sincere, unaffected and wholly amiable.

XLVIII.—Jason

Son of Æson and of Polymede, who was herself the daughter of Autolycus, Jason signifies goodness itself.

1. He thinks that the service is satisfactory.
2. The alteration will please every one.
3. He will die in the highest dignities of his post.
4. Your plans are favoured by Heaven, and your aspirations will be fulfilled.
5. You have none, and they believe that you are ambitious.
6. You may look for nothing but success in this design.
7. He loves you more than you dream.
8. You will have an inconsiderable advantage.
9. There is some appearance of truth in the rumour.
10. Their affection will be of great advantage to them.
11. You will have what you expect and enjoy it at your ease.
12. You have many seeming friends but few true ones.

XLIX.—Theseus

He was the son of Ægeus, King of Athens, and of Æthra, who was a daughter of Pittheus; he should be unto you as a pattern of virtue.

1. His ability is well known; he will become prominent in his present calling.
2. His ambition is to signalise himself still more in the coming year.
3. If you are well off as you are, do not dream of changing.
4. You are born for your position; you will die for it and in it.
5. You will be content and will have your heart's desire.
6. Your ambition is holy.
7. That which is proposed you may welcome with both hands; it is good business for you.
8. He seeks an opportunity to help you.
9. Your good qualities should bring you to a high place in the church.
10. The report is false and is setting many by the ears idly.
11. You will preserve them by your virtue.
12. Ask, pray, and it will be given to you.

L.—Hercules

The son of Jupiter and Alcmena should signify all virtue for you.

1. They will be most virtuous.
2. What should we do without him? He is the first of leaders.
3. He follows the road before him with no sense of responsibility.
4. Discuss your plan for changing with your friends, and be guided by them.
5. God will give you the grace of dying apart from the cares of your business.
6. You will obtain all that you desire.
7. You are he who has least ambition of all the company.
8. Listen to him who speaks; he is impelled by friendship.
9. He wishes you no evil.
10. You will obtain an appointment and will hold it for a long period.
11. There is nothing to shew that the thing happened as people think.
12. Where God reigns all good things also reign.

LI.—Achilles

The son of Thetis and of Peleus, King of Thessaly, should teach you how to overcome.

1. The strongest will bear it away.
2. They will be honest, obliging and will do an ill office to no one.
3. He has been drawn into the service of the State and the State will reward him.
4. There is no reproach against him: his should be a path of glory.
5. Break your bonds: you should have made a change six months ago, and you would have been happy.
6. You will die in harness, and you will remain in lasting memory.
7. You must work yourself on your plan, and then it will succeed.
8. Your ambition is only to get fame.
9. Follow your own counsels prudently; it will be to your great advantage.
10. Do not be anxious: he is not thinking of you.
11. Your friends are seeking to supplant you; you will end by supplanting them.
12. Something will intervene and will make them think or act the contrary.

LII.—Atlas

The son of Japetus and Clymene invites you to think less of earth and more of Heaven.

1. Fear God more, and spare your purse less.
2. Have recourse to Heaven, and you will succeed.
3. They will be rendered ridiculous by their avarice and meanness.
4. This time he will husband his resources, but so only that he may be more liberal later on.
5. He is planning to go into retreat.
6. Learn to despise possessions; you will then be happy as you are and will not seek for change.
7. You are too much attached to earth; you will be cashiered and will not die in your business.
8. Your desires are turned to this world; be less attached thereto.
9. Your ambition is so much the greater as it is so much the more concealed; and yet there are those in the company who are still more ambitious than you.
10. Your avarice will hamper your success in everything.
11. You are altogether indifferent to the person in question.
12. Your life will be long and troublous; you will have no settled appointment.

LIII.—Orpheus

The son of Apollo and Calliope shall accompany his oracles to music.

1. You are too pretty, and are loved accordingly.
2. Affability and flattery will help you to get on.
3. Be careful—you are cajoled; she will prove wanting.
4. They will sham good conduct and pay with fine words.
5. Mistrust will cause them to be discontinued.
6. He looks to make up for past quiet by a round of gaiety at theatres and operas.
7. Wait for a more favourable opportunity to change your condition.
8. Expect to die in retirement; you have given too much good time to business.
9. You carry your wishes too far; they will not be attained.
10. You pass for an ambitious person, but it does not deceive everyone.
11. The person who makes the proposal intends to take you in.
12. He has no evil designs in your respect.

LIV.—Perseus

Seek at the hands of this Hero the knowledge of your destiny in things that belong to heroism.

1. Be more attentive and circumspect: then you will be loved.
2. Your boldness in undertaking anything will make you considered.
3. Push forward fearlessly, and you will attain.
4. The enterprise will succeed well.
5. They will be obliging and honest, but only to gain their ends.
6. A little more compliance and less stubbornness will cause it to go on.
7. He is pondering over a new undertaking.
8. Take care: do nothing unworthy of yourself.
9. You will die in harness.
10. Fortune is in opposition to you; try and win it over.
11. The most ambitious of the whole set is the one who made the proposition.
12. Be prompt: otherwise an unforeseen chance will spoil the project.

LV.—Æsculapius

Son of Apollo and Coronis, the God of Medicine will give you oracles of health.

1. He is too delicate to stand the severity of his station.
2. Leave your present master; his requirements are prejudicial to your constitution.
3. Look after your health, and do not expect to rise higher.
4. By caring for the weal of others as for your own.
5. You are killing yourself; take care: she will not succeed.
6. They will be very sickly.
7. It would be continued, did the constitution allow it.
8. He is planning to return quickly, to get medical advice.
9. Take your doctor with you, if you make any change.
10. You are delicate and require tonics, but do not imagine that you will die.
11. That which you want will come about, but it will not prove to your advantage.
12. You are devoid of ambition, because you are too effeminate.

LVI.—Aristeus

The son of Apollo and Cyrene was God of Shepherds and Peasants: his are oracles of mildness.

1. He will be easy, good-natured and rather womanly.
2. An affection which cannot attain its object will make him change his position.
3. He is too strict for you, and you cannot work together.
4. A distaff would be more suitable than your present occupation.
5. Encourage a few friends who are saying a word in your favour.
6. She will succeed by her sweetness.
7. They will be gallant and lovers of ladies.
8. The civil service would suit him better than the army.
9. He is impatient to see his parents.
10. Your indolence will produce a change for the worse.
11. You will die in your business, but it could be wished that it were otherwise.
12. Supposing you had your wish, it would only prove a misfortune.

LVII.—Prometheus

He stole fire from heaven. The son of Japetus and Clymene gives oracles of many meanings.

1. He will not be welcome, because of his secret and dissimulating mind.
2. He will be lost if he does not leave the country.
3. He will change his vocation shortly.
4. You will never be happy, for you change your masters too often.
5. Your want of aptitude for business will bring you to grief.
6. Be good with the good but not evil with the evil.
7. The opposing party will carry it away.
8. He will be an enemy to peace, notwithstanding his mild ways.
9. It will not continue, because novelty is loved.
10. He is looking for a way to conduct the business.
11. The change should prove your fortune.
12. Be comforted : you will not die there.

LVIII.—Minos

The son of Jupiter and Europa, at one time King of Crete, was made a Judge in Tartarus: may he who was just therein afford you true presages.

1. He will be sorry for whatever he adopts in the first instance.
2. His family and his property will make him welcome.
3. Pride and haughtiness will render him intolerable.
4. He is likely to change his business out of pique.
5. He will have consideration for every one but you.
6. Your ill behaviour alienates those who could advance you.
7. Take more interest in domestic affairs and business.
8. Money will help you to the end in view.
9. Expect no straight dealing on their part: they will bluff everyone.
10. If he stood well with those under him, he would be more likely to go on.
11. He will find it difficult to give account of his undertaking.
12. You have no one to blame but yourself for any evil which follows the change.

LIX.—Rhadamanthus

He was of the same parentage as Minos and filled a similar office in Hades: may he also be true in his forecasts.

1. He will live a long time, but it might be better if he died young.
2. Affliction or disgrace will drive him into utter retirement.
3. He will be welcomed, his real character being unknown.
4. He will be extremely sensitive and a source of trouble thereby.
5. He is likely to throw up his present employment and enter the army.
6. You are too hot-headed and violent to remain under his control.
7. Your care will raise you to a high position in your particular walk.
8. Avoid honours and honours will seek you.
9. The intrigues are too transparent for the thing to succeed.
10. They are too fond of good cheer.
11. It will not go on; his conduct displeases those in power.
12. He is considering which post is likely to prove best for him.

LX.—Charon

He was the son of Erebus and Night, and was the pilot over the river Styx.

1. Your dreams are vain; he will never make a fortune and must look to what he can inherit.

2. He is likely to waste away through maternal inexperience.

3. He will take refuge anywhere from parental severity.

4. He will be respected at first, but when he is known better he is likely to get his *congé*.

5. Before two years, he will turn out different from what was thought.

6. A military career demands courage; get him something to keep the pot boiling.

7. He pretends to have a preference for you, but do not trust him.

8. You are not out of mind; be more willing and agreeable.

9. By changing the method of procedure.

10. She is worthless: why wish her to succeed?

11. They will work for themselves only and make others responsible.

12. He can bring it to no successful issue, and yet is too involved to draw back.

THE ART OF KNOWING THE GOOD GENII

AND THEIR INFLUENCE UPON THE DESTINY OF MEN

THE SECRET DOCTRINE CONCERNING THE THREE GUIDES

ACCORDING to the Secret Doctrine of Cornelius Agrippa, every man has three Guardian Angels or Genii. Of these the first is of Divine rank and order; he comes not in the name of the stars nor with the power of these, but is commissioned by command of God, and the charge of the soul is given him at the time of the soul's creation. This spirit is universal and transcends Nature; he is the rector and governor of life; he imparts Divine Light, or that Light of the Word which enlighteneth every man who cometh into this world; and he lifts up the soul to God.

The second Genius emanates from the astrological world—that is to say, from the power of the stars; he leads man along the path of virtue; his influence is on qualities of the moral order and the things which pass into expression in speech.

The third Genius emanates from the elementary world. He governs the physical part of man; he influences health, motion and actions.

The first Order of Genii operates in the revolution of the 24 hours comprised in each day. The second Order operates in the revolution of the days by which the year is constituted. The third Order operates in the revolution of certain successive periods throughout the year.

The occult philosophy or doctrine of Cornelius Agrippa is based on the Sacred Kabalah, or Secret Tradition of Israel, which postulates 72 Angels or Genii distributed in the above manner through the times and the seasons. It is from this source that we obtain a knowledge of their names, their attributes and their mysteries. These names must not, however, be understood in a limited and personal sense; each of them stands for a host or cohort, a cloud of witnesses, and—as their meanings make evident—a synthesis of supernal powers and graces. It comes about in this manner that the angelical offices are interchangeable; a Genius who governs the physical part of one child that is born on earth is the leader into light of the soul belonging to another, while he presides over the moral qualities and dispositions of a third. It is in this way, and so only, that the influences are calculable and that we can each of us ascertain with facility our own presiding spirits in the tripartite division of our personality, as well as those of others. The more fully we can realise that they are powers, principalities, influences, and that they lead us in proportion as we receive their spirit, the more comprehensive and accurate will be the idea obtained of their prerogative and office.

THE MODE OF EXERCISING THE ART

It is from this standpoint that I proceed to explain the way of ascertaining the Genii who preside over ourselves and those with whom we are connected, either by kinship or acquaintance.

I will assume that you—who are seeking to be a student of this occult art—are anxious to determine these questions in your own case and further that you were born on November 17 at 10.15 a.m. I consult Table I., which follows hereinafter, being the Revolution of the 72 Genii through the 24 hours of the day, and I find that LECABEL rules from 10 in the morning till 10.20 inclusive. It is he therefore who presides over your spiritual part; and by reference to the qualities which belong to his sphere of government, it follows that you should be well equipped in all that belongs to the higher mind. Consult the *Grand Kabalistic Table of the 72 Genii*. According to Table II., the Genius who presides on November 17 is named JERATHEL. It is he therefore who has charge of your moral nature; he will incline you to peace and equity, to science, art and literature. There remains Table III., and I find by reference thereto that VEHUEL, the 49th Genius, rules from November 15 to November 19, both inclusive, and it is he therefore who governs your physical part. It is possible that you belong already to those who are great in this world; but if not, you should remember that his care of your body cannot be exercised without a proportionate influence on the other parts of your personality, and it depends upon you whether under his benign guidance you become distinguished for talent and virtue.

It is in this way that your three Genii work in perfect harmony to insure your welfare, and their offices interpenetrate one another. The same rule obtains throughout the *Grand Kabalistic Table*. For this reason, and seeing also that, as explained already, he who watches over your spirit may have charge of another's moral nature and of a third in his physical nature, you will find that the 72 Genii have offices and a sphere of influence which are catholic to the whole man and not particular only to one or other of his tripartite divisions.

It remains to say that if you are uncertain respecting the moment of your birth, you will no doubt be able to fix the hour itself. Now, according to Table I., three Genii govern each hour successively, ruling for 20 minutes only. Consider therefore your own character and disposition ; then consult the *Grand Kabalistic Table* and decide which of the three Genii is most in correspondence with these.

GRAND KABALISTIC TABLE OF THE SEVENTY-TWO GENII

I. VEHUIAH.—According to its meaning in the sacred tongue, this name announces that God is elevated and exalted above all things. In Christian symbolism, he who bears it and seven who follow hereafter are allocated to the Choir of Seraphim. The person who is born under the rule of this Genius has subtlety, sagacity, capacity for the arts and sciences ; he will be able to undertake and execute the most difficult things ; he will also have military qualifications and abundant energy.

II. JELIEL.—The meaning of this name is the God of succour. The Genius to whom it is ascribed governs kings and princes, maintaining their subjects in obedience. He influences the generation of all beings in the animal kingdom, promotes and restores peace among married people and encourages conjugal fidelity. Those who are born under his presidency have a joyous spirit, agreeable manners, are gallant and devoted to the opposite sex.

III. SITAEL.—The meaning of this name is God the Hope of all creatures. He presides over nobility, magnanimity and the greater occupations of life. The person who is born under his influence loves truth, is a keeper of his word and will help those who are in need of his services. This Genius gives also protection against destroying weapons and wild beasts.

IV. ELEMIAH.—The interpretation of this name is God in His concealment. The Genius who bears it presides over travels, maritime expeditions and useful discoveries. Whosoever is born under his influence will be industrious, fortunate in undertakings and fond of travelling.

V. MAHASIAH.—The meaning of this name is God the Saviour. He governs the transcendental sciences, occult philosophy, theology and the liberal arts. Those who are born under his influence will acquire learning with facility, will be pleasant in disposition and appearance and fond of lawful pleasures.

VI. LELAHEL.—The significance is God

all worthy of praise. This Genius presides over love, fame, sciences, arts and fortune. He who is born under his influence will love to be spoken of and will gain celebrity by his talents and actions.

VII. ACHAIAH.—The meaning of this name is Good and Patient God. The Genius who bears it reigns over patience; he discovers the secrets of Nature; he is active in the spread of light and industry. The person born under his influence will seek instruction in useful matters, will be famous for the successful execution of arduous tasks, and will make useful discoveries in the arts.

VIII. CAHETHEL.—The meaning of this name is Adorable God, and the Genius to whom it belongs presides over agricultural products, particularly those which are necessary to the existence of men and animals. He prompts men to lift up their hearts in gratitude to God for all good things sent down by Him. The person born under his influence will love toil, husbandry, the country and sport. He will be active in all his business.

IX. HAZIEL.—The name signifies God of Mercy, and the Genius to whom it is attributed with seven who follow hereafter, are referred to the Order of Cherubim, according to Christian angelology. He obtains mercy from God, in virtue of which mercy he secures the friendship and favours of the great, as also the fulfilment of a promise which has been made by anyone. He governs good faith and reconciliation. Those who are born under his influence will be sincere in their promises and will forgive those who offend them.

X. ALADIAH.—The meaning of this name is the Propitious God, and the Genius to whom it is allotted exercises his power for the prevention of plagues and the cure of those who are sick. He who is born under his influence will enjoy good health, will be fortunate in his undertakings and will be esteemed by those who know him. He will be welcomed in the highest society.

XI. LAUVIAH.—The name of this Genius signifies : May God be praised and exalted. He is powerful to protect against thunder and to insure victory. He presides over renown, influences the great of this world, the learned and all those who win celebrity by their talents.

XII. HAHAIAH.—The interpretation of this attribute or title is God our refuge. He is the ruler of dreams, and he reveals hidden mysteries to the minds of men. He influences wise, spiritual and discreet people. Those who are born under his dominion are gentle in demeanour, amiable in appearance and pleasant in deportment.

XIII. JEZALEL.—According to the inward meaning of this name, God is glorified in all His works. The Genius who bears it presides over friendship, reconciliation and conjugal fidelity. Those who are born under his influence will learn with ease whatsoever they may seek to acquire. They will have excellent memories and will be distinguished by their tact.

XIV. MEBAHEL.—The message contained in this name is God our Preserver, and the Genius to whom it is assigned rules over justice, truth and freedom. He delivers the oppressed, sets free prisoners, protects innocence and manifests that which is true. Whosoever is born under his influence will love things of the law and may attain distinction at the bar.

XV. HARIEL.—God our Creator is the meaning contained herein, and the Genius whom it designates rules in science and art, influencing useful discoveries and new methods. Those who are born under his government will love the society of all who are true in heart; they will be religious in their feelings and will be distinguished by the purity of their manners.

XVI. HAKAMIAH.—That which is implied in this name is the idea of God as the Maker of the universe. The rule of this Genius is extended over crowned heads and the leaders of armies; he gives victory and warning against seditions; he has charge over arsenals and whatsoever appertains to the art and science of war. The man who is born under his care is frank, loyal and brave, sensitive in matters of honour, faithful to his pledged word and chivalrous towards womanhood.

XVII. LAUVIAH.—The prayer represented by this name is addressed to the Admirable God; the spirit who bears it is referable to the Choir of Thrones and so are seven who come after him in the table of succession which follows. He has dominion over the transcendental sciences, discovers things of wonder and imparts revelations in dream. The person born under his influence will love music, poetry, literature and philosophy.

XVIII. CALIEL.—It is borne witness by this name that God is quick to hear and to grant the prayer of those who put their trust in Him. The Genius who carries this testimony in his title manifests the truth in cases of law, causes the innocent to triumph, confounds the guilty and those who commit perjury. Whosoever is born under his influence will be just, sincere, a lover of truth, and he may attain distinction as a magistrate.

XIX. LEUVIAH.—The significance of this name is the God Who hears sinners, and the Genius whom it distinguishes rules over the understanding and memory of man. The person who is born under his influence will be amiable, modest in speech and simple in mode of life. He will support adversities with resignation and patience.

XX. PAHALIAH. — The bearer of this name, which means Redeeming God, presides over religion, theology and ethics. He promotes chastity, piety and directs those whose vocation is the ecclesiastical state. Those who are born under his influence are meant for the paths of sanctity.

XXI. NELCHAEL.—The interpretation of this name is the One and Only God. The Genius to whom it is attributed presides over astronomy, mathematics, geography and all abstract sciences; philosophers and learned people are under his influence in an especial sense. Those whom he rules from their birth will be lovers of poetry and literature; they will be earnest students and will be distinguished in mathematics and geometry.

XXII. JEIAIEL.—The meaning of this name is Divine Right. The Genius answering thereto rules over fortune, renown, diplomacy and commerce. He influences voyages, discoveries and maritime expeditions; he gives protection against tempests and shipwreck. The person who is born under his influence will be a lover of commerce, industrious and will be distinguished by his liberal and philanthropical ideas.

XXIII. MELAHEL.—The message of this name is God Who delivereth from evil. It is ascribed to a Genius who rules over water, the products of earth and chiefly those plants which have virtue in the cure of diseases. The person who is born under his influence is naturally brave and qualified to lead undertakings, even the most perilous. He will be distinguished also by honourable actions.

XXIV. HAHIUIAH.—The name signifies God Who is Himself goodness, and the Genius to whom it is applied governs those who are in exile and those who are flying from imprisonment, so only that their cause is just. He prevents the discovery of those who are accused untruly. He is also a shield against dangerous animals, as well as thieves and assassins. Whosoever is born under his rule shall love truth and shall be sincere in words and actions. Furthermore, he will be skilled in exact sciences.

XXV. NITH-HAIAH.—This name bears witness to the God Who imparts wisdom. The Genius who bears it as his distinctive title governs all the secret sciences and he affords revelations in dreams, especially to those who are born on a day over which he presides. He influences those wise men who are lovers of peace and solitude, who seek truth and practise the Higher Magia—which is also Divine Magia. This Genius and seven who follow hereafter belong to the Choir of Dominations in the Christian hierarchy of spirits.

XXVI. HAAIAH.—The name of this

Genius testifies to God in His concealment. He is the protection of all those who seek after truth ; he directs men to the contemplation of things divine ; among interests of the external kind he rules in politics and diplomacy, over the offices of plenipotentiaries and embassies, treaties of peace, commercial treaties and all conventions in general. He protects couriers, despatches, agents and secret expeditions.

XXVII. JERATHEL.—The admonition of this name concerns God Who punishes the wicked. The Genius affords protection against those who provoke and attack us without just warrant. He has power in the propagation of light, civilisation and liberty. The person born under his auspices will love peace, equity, science and art. He may become distinguished in literature.

XXVIII. SEHEIAH. — The meaning of this name is God Who heals the sick. The Genius to whom it is given protects against incendiary, destruction of buildings, falls and diseases. He governs health and long life. The person who is born under his auspices will possess much judgment and will act therefore with prudence and circumspection.

XXIX. REIIEL.—The God Who is swift to succour is celebrated by this name. The Genius to whom it is given rules over religious sentiments, divine philosophy and meditation. The person who is born under his influence will be distinguished by virtues and zeal in the propagation of truth ; he will do all in his power to destroy impiety, in writing as well as by his example.

XXX. OMAEL.—The interpretation of this name is God of patience, and the Genius to whom it is ascribed has dominion over the animal kingdom and the perpetuation of species therein. He has charge over chemists, physicians and surgeons. Whosoever is born under his influence will be distinguished in anatomy and medicine.

XXXI. LECABEL.—The testimony which is born by this name is to the Inspiring God. The Genius who bears it rules over vegetation and agriculture. Those who are born on the days referred more especially to him will be devoted to astronomy, mathematics and geometry. They will be distinguished by luminous ideas, will solve the most difficult problems and will owe their fortune to talent.

XXXII. VASARIAH.—The justice of God is saluted in this name, and the Genius to whom it is referred rules over justice and those who represent it on earth—judges, magistrates and advocates. The person born under his influence will be eloquent, amiable, spiritual and modest.

XXXIII. JEHUIAH. — The meaning of this name is God Who knoweth all things. The Genius on whom it is conferred and seven who follow hereafter belong to the Choir of

Powers, according to the orthodox hierarchy of the Blessed Angels. He protects Christian princes and maintains their subjects in obedience. The person who is born under his influence will fulfil faithfully and lovingly the duties of his estate.

XXXIV. LEHAHIAH. — Herein is the praise of the God of Mercy. The Genius who bears this title has government over crowned heads, princes and nobles, maintaining harmony, good understanding and peace between them. He also encourages obedience in subjects towards their princes. Those who are born under his rule will become celebrated by their acts and talents, will earn confidence and favours if they enter the service of the State, and will deserve that which they obtain by their devotion and fidelity.

XXXV. CHAVAKIAH.—The name signifies : God Who is giver of joy. The Genius responding thereto presides over wills, successions and all divisions of property which are performed in harmony. He maintains peace among families. The person born under his influence will live in peace with everyone, even at the sacrifice of his own interests. He will deem it a duty to reward the pains and fidelity of those who are attached to his service.

XXXVI. MENADEL. — The meaning of this name is Adorable God. The Genius to whom it belongs can give news of persons far away, who have not been heard of for long periods of time. He restores exiles to their own country and discovers things that are lost.

XXXVII. ANIEL.—The praise of the God of Virtues is sounded in this name. The Genius confessing thereto presides over sciences and arts; he reveals the secrets of Nature and inspires philosophers in their meditations. The person who is born under his influence will be celebrated for abilities and enlightenment; he will be distinguished among the learned.

XXXVIII. HAAMIAH.—In this name, God is praised as the hope of all the children of men. The Genius adorned therewith governs the official forms of religious worship and all that relates to Divine things, as they are performed here below. He protects the seekers after truth.

XXXIX. REHAEL.—This name is a salutation addressed to that God Who receives sinners. The Genius who bears it presides over health and long life; he maintains, prompts and increases paternal and filial love, with the obedience and respect due from children to their parents.

XL. JEIAZEL. — The meaning of this name is God Who rejoices. The Genius on whom it is conferred presides over printing and the care of books; he guides men of letters and artists. The person born under his influence will love reading, drawing and all the circle of the sciences.

XLI. HAHAHEL.—The testimony borne by this name is to God in Three Persons. The Genius who bears it and seven who follow hereafter belong to the Angelical Choir of Virtues. His power extends over Christendom; he protects missionaries and all disciples of Christ, who preach the Gospel throughout the world. He inspires holy souls, prelates and all persons and things appertaining to the priesthood. Those who are born under his influence will be distinguished by force and greatness of soul; they will be altogether dedicated to the service of God and will suffer martyrdom gladly for Christ's sake.

XLII. MIKAEL.—The following attributions of this name have been furnished by the school of Kabalists: Virtue of God, House of God, Image of God. The Genius to whom it is ascribed has power over kings, princes and nobles; he maintains their subjects in obedience, discovers conspiracies and those who seek to destroy the persons and governments of rulers. Whosoever is born under his influence will be immersed in political affairs; he will be curious, keen to know the secrets of cabinets, eager for strange news, and he will be distinguished in affairs of state by his skill in diplomacy.

XLIII. VEUALIAH.—This name is an invocation of the King Who prevails. The

Genius on whom it is conferred presides over peace and promotes the prosperity of Empires. He strengthens shaking thrones and establishes the power of Kings. The person who is born under his influence will love the profession of arms and desire glory ; he will be constantly engrossed by those sciences which are connected with warfare ; he will become celebrated by his prowess and through such services will win the confidence of his country.

XLIV. JELAHIAH.—The synonym of this title is Eternal God, and it is conferred as a symbol on the Genius who responds thereto. He is the defence against arms, and in this sense he insures victory. Those who are born under him will be drawn to travel for their instruction ; they will succeed in all their enterprises ; they will be famous for military skill and valour ; they will be inscribed on the roll of glory.

XLV. SEALIAH.—The meaning of this name is Mover of all things. The Genius to whom it is given presides over vegetation ; he imparts life and health to all that breathes ; he directs the chief agents of Nature. Those at whose birth he assists will acquire knowledge with gladness ; they will enjoy large resources and many facilities.

XLVI. ARIEL. — The Divine Being is saluted in this name as Revealing God. The Genius who receives it as his endowment discovers concealed treasures, makes known the greatest secrets of Nature and shews desired objects in dream. The person born under his influence is gifted with a strong and subtle spirit; his ideas will be new and sublime; he will solve the most difficult problems; in fine, he will be discreet and will act with great circumspection.

XLVII. ASALIAH.—The hidden grace of this name is called upon as the Just God Which sheweth forth truth, and the Genius to whom it is given presides over justice and manifests the truth in litigation. He inspires the upright and those who lift up their minds to the contemplation of Divine things. The person who is born under his influence is endowed with an agreeable disposition; he will be unweary in his search after secret lights.

XLVIII. MIHAEL. — The Succourable Father and God is celebrated in this name. The Genius on whom it is conferred will protect those who have recourse to him, and he will give them secret presentiments and inspirations on things to come. He presides over generation; he promotes friendship and conjugal love. The person who is born under his influence will be of loving disposition and will be fond of all innocent pleasures.

XLIX. VEHUEL.—The Great and Exalted God is invoked in this name, and the Genius who is sealed therewith presides over the great of this world, but especially over those who are raised up and distinguished for their talents and virtues. He belongs to the Choir of Principalities, with seven who follow hereafter. Whosoever is born under his influence will be of sensible and generous soul; he will be prized for his virtues and good deeds by all who are themselves good; he may be also distinguished in literature, jurisprudence and diplomacy.

L. DANIEL.—The meaning of this name is said to be the Sign of Mercies or, according to others, the Angel of Confessions. The Genius to whom it is ascribed presides over justice, barristers, lawyers and the judicial bench at large. He gives sudden inspirations to those who are embarrassed by alternative courses and do not know how to choose between them. The person who is born under his influence will be industrious in business matters, will be fond of literature and will make a mark by his eloquence.

LI. HAHASIAH.—God in His concealment is signified by this name, and the Genius sealed therewith presides over chemistry and physics; he makes known the greatest secrets of Nature, including the Philosophical Stone and Universal Medicine. The person born under his dominion will have a liking for abstract sciences; he will investigate the properties and virtues attributed to animals, vegetables and minerals; as a physician, he will be distinguished for extraordinary cures, and in this and other walks he will make discoveries useful to society.

LII. IMAMIAH.—The hidden grace of this name testifies to God Who is exalted above all that is. The Genius to whom it is attributed presides over voyages in general; he protects prisoners who have recourse to him and inspires their minds as to the ways of obtaining liberty. He prompts those who seek truth sincerely and those who after their errors return with all their hearts to God. The person who is born under his influence will be endowed with strength of character; he will support adversity with patience and courage; he will love work and will execute with facility whatever he decides to undertake.

LIII. NANAEL.—We are reminded by this name that God humbles pride. The Genius to whom it is allotted presides over the higher sciences; he is the guide of ecclesiastics, professors, magistrates and men of law. Those who are born under his influence will be reserved in disposition; they will prefer private life, repose and meditation; they will be distinguished by their attainments in the abstract sciences.

LIV. NITHAEL. — The inward meaning of this name offers salutation to the King of Heaven. The Genius who bears it as his title presides over emperors, kings, princes, and all civil and sacerdotal dignities. He has the charge of legitimate dynasties and the stability of empires; he gives a long and peaceful reign to the potentates who have recourse to him and protects those who seek to maintain their official or business positions. Whosoever is born under his influence will become famous for his writings and eloquence; he will have a high reputation among the learned, will be distinguished for his virtues and will deserve public confidence.

LV. MEBAHIAH.—The meaning of this name offers an invocation to the Eternal God. The Genius who receives it as his title presides over morals and religion; he guides those who maintain both with all their power. The person who is born under his rule will be distinguished by good actions, piety and zeal in the discharge of his duties towards God and man.

LVI. POIEL.—The concealed meaning of this name offers praise to that God Who sustains the universe. The Genius to whom it belongs presides over renown, fortune and philosophy. He who is born under his dominion will be esteemed by all for his modesty, moderation and amiable disposition; his fortune in life will be due to his talents and conduct.

LVII. NEMAMIAH. — The meaning of this name testifies to God Who is worthy of all praise. The Genius on whom it is conferred rules over leaders of armies, admirals and all those who sustain a just cause in warfare. He belongs to the Choir of Archangels, with seven who follow hereafter. The person who is born under his influence will find his vocation in the profession of arms; he will be distinguished for his energy, bravery and grandeur of soul; he will support hardships with courage.

LVIII. IEIALEL.—The God Who hears the generations is invoked in this name. The Genius who bears it has all iron under his government and all implements which are formed of this metal. He presides also over those who work in iron or deal commercially therein. He confounds the wicked and bearers of false testimony. Whosoever is born under his influence will be distinguished by frankness and boldness. He will be also great in love.

LIX. HARAHEL.—The inward meaning of this name is a prayer addressed to that God Who knows all things. The Genius who bears it presides over treasures, houses of exchange, public funds, archives, libraries and depositories of precious things. He influences printing, publishing and those who deal therein. The person who is born under his dominion will acquire knowledge with eagerness; his pursuits and interests will be numerous; he will follow stock operations, will be successful in speculation, but will be distinguished by his probity as well as by talents and fortune.

LX. MITZRAEL.—It is testified by this name that God comforts the oppressed. The Genius to whom it is referable presides over those who are distinguished by their talents and virtues ; he promotes the obedience of inferiors to those who are placed over them. The person who is born under his influence will combine the best qualities of body and soul ; he will be eminent by his virtues, his mental qualities and pleasant disposition. His days will be long in the land.

LXI. UMABEL.—The Praise of the God above all things is recited in this name. The Genius on whom it is conferred presides over astronomy and physics, as over those who are dedicated to these subjects. Whoever is born under this government will love travelling and all honourable pleasures ; he will have a feeling heart and may be wounded in love.

LXII. JAH-HEL.—The hidden sense of this name offers homage to the Supreme Being. The Genius whose title it is presides over the philosophies, the *Illuminati,* and those who would retire from the world. The person who is born under his influence will love tranquillity and solitude ; he will fulfil the duties of his state faithfully and will be distinguished by his modesty and virtues.

LXIII. ANAUEL.—The God Who is infinitely good is saluted in this name. The Genius to whom it belongs protects against accidents, preserves health and cures diseases. He presides over commerce, bankers, business agents and commissaries. The person who is born under his rule will be of subtle and ingenious mind ; he will be characterised by his industry and activity.

LXIV. MEHIEL.—The hidden grace of this word offers homage to God Who vivifies all things, and the Genius who bears it is a shield against wild beasts. He presides over scholars, professors, orators and authors ; he influences printing, publishing and those who trade in these. The person born under his government will be distinguished in literature.

LXV. DAMABIAH.—The meaning of this name proclaims that God is the Fountain of Wisdom. The Genius to whom it is ascribed and those who follow hereafter belong to the Choir of Angels, or ninth Celestial Hierarchy. He presides over seas, rivers, springs, maritime expeditions and naval constructions. He has charge of mariners, pilots and fishermen, as also over those who deal in fish and industries connected with the sea. Whosoever is born under his influence will be distinguished by maritime expeditions and discoveries, in which he will make a considerable fortune.

LXVI. MANAKEL.—The meaning of this name is that God supports and nourishes all things. The Genius allocated thereto presides over marine vegetation and animals. He has power in sleep and dreams. Whosoever is born under his influence will unite the best qualities of soul and body; he will gain the goodwill and affection of all men of goodwill, owing to the amiability and sweetness of his character.

LXVII. EIAEL.—According to this name, God is the delight of the sons of men. The Genius who is sealed thereby presides over changes, the preservation of monuments and length of days; he has power in the occult sciences; and he will manifest truth to those who seek him in their labours. The person who is born under his influence will love solitude and will be distinguished in the higher branches of knowledge—especially in astronomy, physics and philosophy.

LXVIII. HABUHIAH.—It is testified by this name that God is a generous Giver, and the Genius who bears it presides over agriculture and fruitfulness. Whosoever is born under his influence will love country life, gardens, hunting and all that appertains to agriculture.

LXIX. ROCHEL.—The meaning of this name is God Who beholds all. The Genius on whom it is conferred has dominion over renown, fortune and inheritances; he presides over judges, magistrates, solicitors, pleaders and notaries. Whosoever is born under his influence will attain eminence at the bar through his acquaintance with the laws, manners and customs of all nations.

LXX. JABAMIAH. — The equivalent of this name is the Word which produces all things. The Genius whose title it is presides over the generation of beings and over natural phenomena. He protects those who seek regeneration and to restore within them the harmony broken by the disobedience of Adam. This is accomplished by elevation of the soul to God and by the purification of those elements which enter into the constitution of man. The wise man returns thereby into the principle of creation; he recovers his original dignity and rights; he becomes master of Nature and enjoys the prerogatives bestowed by God on the human race at its creation. The person who is born under the rule of this Genius will be distinguished by his capacities; he will be held learned among all peoples and will become a high light of philosophy.

LXXI. HAIAIEL.—The testimony borne by this name is to God as the Master of the Universe. The Genius to whom it is given protects those who have recourse to him; he gives victory and peace; he has power over iron, arsenals, fortified towns and all that belongs to the art of war. The person who is born under his influence will be endowed with great energy; he will have the military vocation and will be distinguished by his bravery, talents and activity.

LXXII. MUMIAH.—The synonym of this name is found in the letter *Omega,* which signifies the end of all things. The Genius who bears this title gives protection in mysterious operations, insures success in undertakings and leads experiments to their completion. He presides over chemistry, physics and medicine, imparts health and long life. Whosoever is born under his influence will become famous in medicine, will be celebrated for wonderful cures, will discover many secrets of Nature, which will be for the welfare of the children of earth, and will consecrate his vigils and his cares to relieve the poor and sick.

SECRET DOCTRINE OF THE INFLUENCE EXERCISED BY THE 72 GENII OVER THE PERSONALITY OF MAN

I have explained that the Genii recognised by Kabalistic Doctrine are principles, powers and influences rather than individual spirits. They have been sometimes represented as governing different nations of the earth. In this sense VEHUIAH is the Genius of the Hebrews, IEIAIEL that of the English and LECABEL that of the Chinese. They have been allocated to great intellectual classes. In this sense NITH-HAIAH is the Genius of the Magi, HAAMIAH of the Kabalists, DAMABIAH of the Gymnosophists and ANIEL of philosophers in general. The allocation obtains in the latter rather than in the former series; but it has to be understood that all the presiding influences are universal rather than particular, essentially and in themselves, though they may be and are individualised in us, by our dedication to those subjects, affairs and interests over which they preside. As principles and influences, they are distributed over the whole world, and it is necessary to repeat that in their government of human personality the Genius who rules the physical part of James, Wilfred and John may be set over the moral nature of Roland, Oliver and Lancelot, but over the soul and spirit of Alexander, Gregory and Basil. This is explained by the doctrine that certain powers, qualities, or—if you will—Genii are allocated (*a*) to the hours of the day, (*b*) to days recurring throughout the year in a defined succession, and (*c*) to days of the month. These modes of classification are postulates of the doctrine, are a tradition which comes down from the past and stand at their own value as formulations of occult law. Of the law itself there is no explanation; like other laws, it is imposed and must be taken on trust by all who are concerned in the matter.

There arise in this manner three Kabalistic tabulations as they follow hereinafter.

TABLE I.—Revolution of the 72 Genii through the 24 Hours of the Day, revealing the Genius who Governs the Spirit and Soul of Man according to his Hour of Birth.

1. VEHUIAH rules from 12 midnight to 12.20 a.m.

2. JELIEL rules from 12.20 a.m. to 12.40 a.m.

3. SITAEL rules from 12.40 a.m. to 1 a.m.

4. ELEMIAH rules from 1 a.m. to 1.20 a.m.

5. MAHASIAH rules from 1.20 a.m. to 1.40 a.m.

6. LELAHEL rules from 1.40 a.m. to 2 a.m.

7. ACHAIAH rules from 2 a.m. to 2.20 a.m.

8. CAHETHEL rules from 2.20 a.m. to 2.40 a.m.

9. HAZIEL rules from 2.40 a.m. to 3 a.m.

10. ALADIAH rules from 3 a.m. to 3.20 a.m.

11. LAUVIAH rules from 3.20 a.m. to 3.40 a.m.

12. HAHAIAH rules from 3.40 a.m. to 4 a.m.

13. JEZALEL rules from 4 a.m. to 4.20 a.m.

14. MEBAHEL rules from 4.20 a.m. to 4.40 a.m.

15. HARIEL rules from 4.40 a.m. to 5 a.m.

16. HAKAMIAH rules from 5 a.m. to 5.20 a.m.

17. LAUVIAH rules from 5.20 a.m. to 5.40 a.m.

18. CALIEL rules from 5.40 a.m. to 6 a.m.

19. LEUVIAH rules from 6 a.m. to 6.20 a.m.

20. PAHALIAH rules from 6.20 a.m. to 6.40 a.m.

21. NELCHAEL rules from 6.40 a.m. to 7 a.m.

22. JEIAIEL rules from 7 a.m. to 7.20 a.m.

23. MELAHEL rules from 7.20 a.m. to 7.40 a.m.

24. HAHIUIAH rules from 7.40 a.m. to 8 a.m.

25. NITH-HAIAH rules from 8 a.m. to 8.20 a.m.

26. HAAIAH rules from 8.20 a.m. to 8.40 a.m.

27. JERATHEL rules from 8.40 a.m. to 9 a.m.

28. SEHEIAH rules from 9 a.m. to 9.20 a.m.

29. REIIEL rules from 9.20 a.m. to 9.40 a.m.

30. OMAEL rules from 9.40 a.m. to 10 a.m.

31. LECABEL rules from 10 a.m. to 10.20 a.m.

32. VASARIAH rules from 10.20 a.m. to 10.40 a.m.

33. JEHUIAH rules from 10.40 a.m. to 11 a.m.

34. LEHAHIAH rules from 11 a.m. to 11.20 a.m.

35. CHAVAKIAH rules from 11.20 a.m. to 11.40 a.m.

36. MENADEL rules from 11.40 a.m. to 12 noon.

37. ANIEL rules from 12 noon to 12.20 p.m.

38. HAAMIAH rules from 12.20 p.m. to 12.40 p.m.

39. REHAEL rules from 12.40 p.m. to 1 p.m.

40. JEIAZEL rules from 1 p.m. to 1.20 p.m.

41. HAHAHEL rules from 1.20 p.m. to 1.40 p.m.

42. MIKAEL rules from 1.40 p.m. to 2 p.m.

43. VEUALIAH rules from 2 p.m. to 2.20 p.m.

44. JELAHIAH rules from 2.20 p.m. to 2.40 p.m.

45. SEALIAH rules from 2.40 p.m. to 3 p.m.

46. ARIEL rules from 3 p.m. to 3.20 p.m.

47. ASALIAH rules from 3.20 p.m. to 3.40 p.m.

48. MIHAEL rules from 3.40 p.m. to 4 p.m.

49. VEHUEL rules from 4 p.m. to 4.20 p.m.

50. DANIEL rules from 4.20 p.m. to 4.40 p.m.

51. HAHASIAH rules from 4.40 p.m. to 5 p.m.

52. IMAMIAH rules from 5 p.m. to 5.20 p.m.

53. NANAEL rules from 5.20 p.m. to 5.40 p.m.

54. NITHAEL rules from 5.40 p.m. to 6 p.m.

55. MEBAHIAH rules from 6 p.m. to 6.20 p.m.

56. POIEL rules from 6.20 p.m. to 6.40 p.m.

57. NEMAMIAH rules from 6.40 p.m. to 7 p.m.

58. IEIALEL rules from 7 p.m. to 7.20 p.m.

59. HARAHEL rules from 7.20 p.m. to 7.40 p.m.

60. MITZRAEL rules from 7.40 p.m. to 8 p.m.

61. UMABEL rules from 8 p.m. to 8.20 p.m.

62. JAH-HEL rules from 8.20 p.m. to 8.40 p.m.

63. ANAUEL rules from 8.40 p.m. to 9 p.m.

64. MEHIEL rules from 9 p.m. to 9.20 p.m.

65. DAMABIAH rules from 9.20 p.m. to 9.40 p.m.

66. MANAKEL rules from 9.40 p.m. to 10 p.m.

67. EIAEL rules from 10 p.m. to 10.20 p.m.

68. HABUHIAH rules from 10.20 p.m. to 10.40 p.m.

69. ROCHEL rules from 10.40 p.m. to 11 p.m.

70. JABAMIAH rules from 11 p.m. to 11.20 p.m.

71. HAIAIEL rules from 11.20 p.m. to 11.40 p.m.

72. MUMIAH rules from 11.40 p.m. to 12 midnight.

TABLE II.—Revolutions of the 72 Genii through the 12 Months of the Year, revealing the Genius who governs the Moral Nature of Man, according to the Day of his Birth.

1. VEHUIAH rules on March 20, May 31, August 11, October 22 and January 2.

2. JELIEL rules on March 21, June 1, August 12, October 23 and January 3.

3. SITAEL rules on March 22, June 2, August 13, October 24 and January 4.

4. ELEMIAH rules on March 23, June 3, August 14, October 25 and January 5.

5. MAHASIAH rules on March 24, June 4, August 15, October 26 and January 6.

6. LELAHEL rules on March 25, June 5, August 16, October 27 and January 7.

7. ACHAIAH rules on March 26, June 6, August 17, October 28 and January 8.

8. CAHETHEL rules on March 27, June 7, August 18, October 29 and January 9.

9. HAZIEL rules on March 28, June 8, August 19, October 30 and January 10.

10. ALADIAH rules on March 29, June 9, August 20, October 31 and January 11.

11. LAUVIAH rules on March 30, June 10, August 21, November 1 and January 12.

12. HAHAIAH rules on March 31, June 11, August 22, November 2 and January 13.

13. JEZALEL rules on April 1, June 12, August 23, November 3 and January 14.

14. MEBAHEL rules on April 2, June 13, August 24, November 4 and January 15.

15. HARIEL rules on April 3, June 14, August 25, November 5 and January 16.

16. HAKAMIAH rules on April 4, June 15, August 26, November 6 and January 17.

17. LAUVIAH rules on April 5, June 16, August 27, November 7 and January 18.

18. CALIEL rules on April 6, June 17, August 28, November 8 and January 19.

19. LEUVIAH rules on April 7, June 18, August 29, November 9 and January 20.

20. PAHALIAH rules on April 8, June 19, August 30, November 10 and January 21.

21. NELCHAEL rules on April 9, June 20, August 31, November 11 and January 22.

22. JEIAIEL rules on April 10, June 21, September 1, November 12 and January 23.

23. MELAHEL rules on April 11, June 22, September 2, November 13 and January 24.

24. HAHIUIAH rules on April 12, June 23, September 3, November 14 and January 25.

25. NITH-HAIAH rules on April 13, June 24, September 4, November 15 and January 26.

26. HAAIAH rules on April 14, June 25, September 5, November 16 and January 27.

27. JERATHEL rules on April 15, June 26, September 6, November 17 and January 28.

28. SEHEIAH rules on April 16, June 27, September 7, November 18 and January 29.

29. REIIEL rules on April 17, June 28, September 8, November 19 and January 30.

30. OMAEL rules on April 18, June 29, September 9, November 20 and January 31.

31. LECABEL rules on April 19, June 30, September 10, November 21 and February 1.

32. VASARIAH rules on April 20, July 1, September 11, November 22 and February 2.

33. JEHUIAH rules on April 21, July 2, September 12, November 23 and February 3.

34. LEHAHIAH rules on April 22, July 3, September 13, November 24 and February 4.

35. CHAVAKIAH rules on April 23, July 4, September 14, November 25 and February 5.

36. MENADEL rules on April 24, July 5, September 15, November 26 and February 6.

37. ANIEL rules on April 25, July 6, September 16, November 27 and February 7.

38. HAAMIAH rules on April 26, July 7, September 17, November 28 and February 8.

39. REHAEL rules on April 27, July 8, September 18, November 29 and February 9.

40. JEIAZEL rules on April 28, July 9, September 19, November 30 and February 10.

41. HAHAHEL rules on April 29, July 10, September 20, December 1 and February 11.

42. MIKAEL rules on April 30, July 11, September 21, December 2 and February 12.

43. VEUALIAH rules on May 1, July 12, September 22, December 3 and February 13.

44. JELAHIAH rules on May 2, July 13, September 23, December 4 and February 14.

45. SEALIAH rules on May 3, July 14, September 24, December 5 and February 15.

46. ARIEL rules on May 4, July 15, September 25, December 6 and February 16.

47. ASALIAH rules on May 5, July 16, September 26, December 7 and February 17.

48. MIHAEL rules on May 6, July 17, September 27, December 8 and February 18.

49. VEHUEL rules on May 7, July 18, September 28, December 9 and February 19.

50. DANIEL rules on May 8, July 19, September 29, December 10 and February 20.

51. HAHASIAH rules on May 9, July 20, September 30, December 11 and February 21.

52. IMAMIAH rules on May 10, July 21, October 1, December 12 and February 22.

53. NANAEL rules on May 11, July 22, October 2, December 13 and February 23.

54. NITHAEL rules on May 12, July 23, October 3, December 14 and February 24.

55. MEBAHIAH rules on May 13, July 24, October 4, December 15 and February 25.

56. POIEL rules on May 14, July 25, October 5, December 16 and February 26.

57. NEMAMIAH rules on May 15, July 26, October 6, December 17 and February 27.

58. IEIALEL rules on May 16, July 27, October 7, December 18 and February 28.

59. HARAHEL rules on May 17, July 28, October 8, December 19 and March 1.

60. MITZRAEL rules on May 18, July 29, October 9, December 20 and March 2.

61. UMABEL rules on May 19, July 30, October 10, December 21 and March 3.

62. JAH-HEL rules on May 20, July 31, October 11, December 22 and March 4.

63. ANAUEL rules on May 21, August 1, October 12, December 23 and March 5.

64. MEHIEL rules on May 22, August 2, October 13, December 24 and March 6.

65. DAMABIAH rules on May 23, August 3, October 14, December 25 and March 7.

66. MANAKEL rules on May 24, August 4, October 15, December 26 and March 8.

67. EIAEL rules on May 25, August 5, October 16, December 27 and March 9.

68. HABUHIAH rules on May 26, August 6, October 17, December 28 and March 10.

69. ROCHEL rules on May 27, August 7, October 18, December 29 and March 11.

70. JABAMIAH rules on May 28, August 8, October 19, December 30 and March 12.

71. HAIAIEL rules on May 29, August 9, October 20, December 31 and March 13.

72. MUMIAH rules on May 30, August 10, October 21, January 1 and March 14.

It will be observed that between March 14 which terminates rule of MUMIAH and March 20 which begins that of VEHUIAH at the opening of the above Table, there is a space of 5 days not taken into account, and this is the case also with the Table which next follows. Four of these days are referred by Kabalism to certain Intelligences of the Four Elements, while the fifth is consecrated to God. When the year is bi-sextile—that is to say, when it is a leap year, there is a sixth day, which is attributed to the higher spirit of man as the vicegerent of God on earth. The system with which I am dealing is silent on the subject, but it must be understood that people who are born on one of these six days will have the three angels belonging to their birth-hour as guardians of the three parts of their personality. Thus, he who enters this life on February 29 in a leap year, between 2 and 3 in the morning, will have ACHIAH ruling his spirit and soul, CAHETHEL presiding over his moral nature, and HAZIEL over his physical body.

TABLE III.—Revolutions of the 72 Genii through the Days of the Months, revealing the Genius who governs the physical nature of Man, according to the Day of his Birth.

1. VEHUIAH rules from March 20 to March 24, both inclusive.
2. JELIEL rules from March 25 to March 29.
3. SITAEL rules from March 30 to April 3.
4. ELEMIAH rules from April 4 to April 8.
5. MAHASIAH rules from April 9 to April 13.
6. LELAHEL rules from April 14 to April 18.
7. ACHAIAH rules from April 19 to April 23.
8. CAHETHEL rules from April 24 to April 28.
9. HAZIEL rules from April 29 to May 3.
10. ALADIAH rules from May 4 to May 8.

11. LAUVIAH rules from May 9 to May 13.

12. HAHAIAH rules from May 14 to May 18.

13. JEZALEL rules from May 19 to May 23.

14. MEBAHEL rules from May 24 to May 28.

15. HARIEL rules from May 29 to June 2.

16. HAKAMIAH rules from June 3 to June 7.

17. LAUVIAH rules from June 8 to June 12.

18. CALIEL rules from June 13 to June 17.

19. LEUVIAH rules from June 18 to June 22.

20. PAHALIAH rules from June 23 to June 27.

21. NELCHAEL rules from June 28 to July 2.

22. JEIAIEL rules from July 3 to July 7.

23. MELAHEL rules from July 8 to July 12.

24. HAHIUIAH rules from July 13 to July 17.

25. NITH-HAIAH rules from July 18 to July 22.

26. HAAIAH rules from July 23 to July 27.

27. JERATHEL rules from July 28 to August 1.

28. SEHEIAH rules from August 2 to August 6.

29. REIIEL rules from August 7 to August 11.

30. OMAEL rules from August 12 to August 16.

31. LECABEL rules from August 17 to August 21.

32. VASARIAH rules from August 22 to August 26.

33. JEHUIAH rules from August 27 to August 31.

34. LEHAHIAH rules from September 1 to September 5.

35. CHAVAKIAH rules from September 6 to September 10.

36. MENADEL rules from September 11 to September 15.

37. ANIEL rules from September 16 to September 20.

38. HAAMIAH rules from September 21 to September 25.

39. REHAEL rules from September 26 to September 30.

40. JEIAZEL rules from October 1 to October 5.

41. HAHAHEL rules from October 6 to October 10.

42. MIKAEL rules from October 11 to October 15.

43. VEUALIAH rules from October 16 to October 20.

44. JELAHIAH rules from October 21 to October 25.

45. SEALIAH rules from October 26 to October 30.

46. ARIEL rules from October 31 to November 4.

47. ASALIAH rules from November 5 to November 9.

48. MIHAEL rules from November 9 to November 14.

49. VEHUEL rules from November 15 to November 19.

50. DANIEL rules from November 20 to November 24.

51. HAHASIAH rules from November 25 to November 29.

52. IMAMIAH rules from November 30 to December 4.

53. NANAEL rules from December 5 to December 9.

54. NITHAEL rules from December 10 to December 14.

55. MEBAHIAH rules from December 15 to December 19.

56. POIEL rules from December 20 to December 24.

57. NEMAMIAH rules from December 25 to December 29.

58. IEIALEL rules from December 30 to January 3.

59. HARAHEL rules from January 4 to January 8.

60. MITZRAEL rules from January 9 to January 13.

61. UMABEL rules from January 14 to January 18.

62. JAH-HEL rules from January 19 to January 23.

63. ANAUEL rules from January 24 to January 28.

64. MEHIEL rules from January 29 to February 2.

65. DAMABIAH rules from February 3 to February 7.

66. MANAKEL rules from February 8 to February 12.

67. EIAEL rules from February 13 to February 17.

68. HABUHIAH rules from February 18 to February 22.

69. ROCHEL rules from February 23 to February 27.

70. JABAMIAH rules from February 28 to March 4.

71. HAIAIEL rules from March 5 to March 9.

72. MUMIAH rules from March 10 to March 14.

THE MYSTERY OF GRACE AND ATTAINMENT CONCEALED IN THIS ART

It is an old Kabalistic doctrine that the whole creation is permeated and stayed up by the virtues and graces of the Divine Names, which are to be understood in no arbitrary sense—as if words or names *per se* possessed an inherent potency—but as representing attributes of the Infinite Being. They are like openings in the abyss of Deity, through which we perceive in the uplifting of our limited faculties some aspects of God in His manifestation. The greatest of all Names is יהוה, *Yod, He, Vau, He,* rendered by us as Jehovah—the permutations of which are innumerable. The utmost expansion of this Name extends to 72 letters and is called שמהמפורש, *Shemhamphorash,* being the word expounded in its fulness. The titles of the 72 Angels, with whose qualities and offices I have been dealing, connect therewith and therefore the Name Jehovah is the power of all, even as it is the source of each. Their titles are indeed His attributes, and so far as we regard them in the personal sense, the reader will understand that they are acting only as Divine Vicegerents, whether in the world without or the inward world of our humanity. Through them, for this reason, we can direct our eyes to the Centre and by the means of attainments which they represent, we may hope to reach the Centre. If VEHUIAH, the first Angel, governs our spiritual part, according to the Mystic Calendar of Kabalism and according to our birth-date, it means that God will uplift those who are dedicated in the soul to Him till they acquire that subtlety of spirit by which all grossness can be purged from the entire personality and the veils thus removed which hinder our communion with the Divine. We can become moreover on earth the faithful soldiers of the Most High, which is the mystic sense of the Martial influence connected with the particular angelic office, while the fire which also belongs thereto is that zeal for the House of God and for His Holy Place which is said to eat up the Postulant who goes forth on the quest of Him.

The 36th Angel is MENADEL, who is said to restore exiles to their native land. Should the period of our birth indicate that he has the care of our moral nature, let us so harmonise our life that the providence which he represents in God and the worship of the Adorable God may bring us under the everlasting wings, so that we may be taken in fine out of prison, from the exile of mortal life, and brought into our true country—world of the life of life and home of souls. The Divine Maxim ascribed to the 36th Angel is: "I have loved, O Lord, the beauty of Thy House and the place where Thy Glory dwelleth."

If MUMIAH, the 72nd Angel, has rule over our physical part, according to the witness of our nativity, this signifies—under Divine Providence—that those who perform the work referred to the charge of this spirit may look for long life in the manifest land of the living, so that their vocation may be carried to its completion. It is not a guarantee of long life but a recognition of the principle that what God has given us to do, He will enable us to fulfil in His name. We shall lack not the time for His service. On those who have healing power and skill in medical science there is imposed the duty of caring for the poor and needy, the widowed and the orphaned, in the necessity of sickness; and Nature will open at need the secrets of her glorious operations to the ministers who obey the call. But we must remember through all that our earthly life has its *Alpha* and *Omega*, its beginning and end; that the *Alpha* was a work of God in the incarnation here below of our spirits which derive from above; and that the end must be even as the beginning, as in Him Who is the term of all.

The other offices are to be understood after the same manner and every serious student can interpret them for his own enlightenment, his encouragement in the true way of Divine and Human Science. The power which presides over physical generation will recall to him the second birth and the regenerated life to which it is the door set open. If we take what will seem to be the lowest and most external offices, the power which protects us against offensive weapons and the attacks of wild beasts will remind us that the keenest swords and the most ravening creatures of prey are in our own untutored hearts ; the diseases against which other powers are deputed to defend us are shadows only of the sickness and plagues of the soul ; the expeditions, the discoveries, the voyages which are ruled by yet others are veils of the soul's travellings. We can derive, in this manner, out of all, the counsels of the Angel of Great Counsel, the wisdom of the Prince of Peace and so prepare for that priesthood which is in the care of HAHAHEL, the 41st Angel, for this in its highest aspect is the priesthood not imposed with hands, but eternal in the heavens and according to the Order of Melchisidech.

THE OCCULT SCIENCE OF JEWELS

THE SYMBOLISM OF PRECIOUS STONES

THERE is assuredly a language of gems, as there is that of flowers, but the beautiful and the precious stones, precious for our purpose in proportion to their beauty, are few in comparison with the jewels of the floral world. I think on my own part that their speech is sometimes deeper ; the Ruby has abysses of meaning, and I do not know where it is possible to find in Nature a greater talisman than the Carbuncle. It is difficult to take these and the other wonders and glories with which I am about to deal and not feel that, even in the Science of the Magi, we have touched only the fringe of their mysteries. They open worlds to contemplation which are comparable to the human heart ; and the reason—as it seems to me—is that in each bright stone, " the eye that contemplates it well, perceives " the unplumbed self therein. It is in this respect like the stars, the sea, the great pageant of creation. The Magi say that we are made in the likeness of the universe, and it is for this reason that we read ourselves therein. In precious stones we read our own thoughts and emotions, so there is one sense at least in which the virtues that we attribute to them are transferred from ourselves. But the law of correspondence between the greater world about us and the lesser world within should teach us that the virtues are in both, that they speak one to another, hold up the glass to each other, act and react on one another, having a sympathetic bond in common.

We are symbols to ourselves because we are known only in part by ourselves, and our manifest being is only a sign, omen, or shadow of the infinite behind us. It is the same with flowers, the same also with jewels; and though in the pages which follow I have collected much that is of meaning from the annals of old-world lore, the reader who has gifts of discernment can learn, should he choose, for himself that the true art of the subject has never been put into writing, that he must read in the stones himself, and then he will find those "thoughts that do often lie too deep for tears"—and far too deep for words. He will learn also in what sense the virtues attributed to gems may sometimes be understood literally, but often—and much more often—in a mystic and interior way. They would not be symbols if their meanings were not also symbolic.

THE ROSARY OF PRECIOUS STONES

Agate

This is really a generic name, including many varieties of stones to which special names, qualities and virtues are attributed. The word is said to be derived from the river Achates in Sicily, where Agates were found in abundance; but this was in the old classical days, when they were used for engraving cameos and intaglios. The folk-lore of precious stones tells us that the Agate is the stone of the planet Jupiter, but talismanic Kabalism refers it to the influence of Mercury, wherein is the gift of counsel and presidency over several liberal arts—eloquence, poetry, music, astronomy, mathematics, and the professors of these. Generally speaking, the Agate signifies joy, courage, happiness and prosperity. It fortifies the heart against the warfare of life. It is a cure for the bites of wild beasts, scorpions and poisonous spiders. It is also a preservative against plague. He who carries an Agate does not suffer from thirst, and his sight is strengthened. It conduces to gaiety, wreathes the lips with smiles and is favourable to health. It is in equal sympathy with those who are happy and in misfortune.

Amber

Many tender legends and beliefs of the older world have gathered about this transparent substance, which in the perfection of its clouded state is still as a gift of the gods, but to those mostly or only who have been initiated, passed and raised in the mysteries of tobacco. It signifies beauty and sweetness and it was called in antiquity Tears of Brotherhood, indurated and aureated by the sun. It was said also—to account for its origin—that the daughters of Apollo were so grief-stricken at the death of their brother Phæton that the gods changed them into poplars, so that their sorrow might be forgotten. It came about, however, that they remembered, and beautiful tears of Amber exuded from the barks. It is true that the substance is of vegetable origin, but it comes from no living tree; it is the last transformation of antediluvian conifers. It exhales an aromatic, resinous perfume in burning, and as it entered into the composition of that incense which was offered before the Tabernacle by command of Moses, so at a later day it was burnt in the mosques at Mecca. As it resists all contamination, it was supposed to preserve against secret poison; it has also the mystic power of attracting the sympathy of others towards those who wear it. According to the old-world lore of medicine, it is a preventive of goitre and a cure for dysentery. There was also a mode of its preparation so that it might be taken internally. It was ground into powder and mixed with honey and oil of roses: then it was of service in deafness. When mixed with honey only it was helpful in dimness of sight. But the last state of him who tried these experiments might well be worse than the disease.

Amethyst

This, in the higher language of symbolism, is one of the twelve stones of the Mystic City, and it was also one of those which adorned the pectoral of the Jewish High Priest. In the myths of antiquity it is ascribed variously. Divinatory Kabalism refers it to the planet Mars, wherein is the gift of force, though its influence is operative also in peace, friendship, sincerity and grandeur of soul. Some ancient writers have called it the Stone of Venus; for them it attracts to a man the love of the woman who is beloved by him. But others, and the greater number, say that it was sacred to Bacchus, and its most celebrated occult virtue is as a safeguard against intoxication. So it had a place in the garland of roses which the Roman host presented to each of his guests on taking their seats at a banquet. I do not know whether it so remained throughout the length of the feast, for another story says that at the first signs of drunkenness, the Amethyst should be placed on the centre of the stomach, that it may draw the fumes of wine in that direction, and so relieve the head. It acted also as a preventive, says one more authority in legend, since he who wore it lost the desire to drink, which does not seem to have been the experience at feasts like those of Trimalcyon, nor could it have been with such intention that it was added to the crowns of flowers. But in any case it had higher virtues, for it drove away evil thoughts, promoted chastity, attracted the favour of the great, repelled sorceries, banished sadness of spirit, and among married women exercised a mysterious office in making the barren fruitful. Against all these wonders on the side of things favourable it is suggested only that it occasions unhappy dreams. According to Christian lore, an Amethyst adorned the ring given by St Joseph to the Blessed Virgin on the day of their espousals, and under the obedience of the Latin Rite the church still presents an Amethyst ring to each bishop on his enthronement.

Ammonite

I do not pretend to identify this stone, the name of which suggests a meteoric origin, but I have heard of an occult variety called the Horn of Ammon—who was a horned Deity—and this should be worth seeking, for those who place it under the pillow at night will have prophetic or divine dreams. Prophecies may be of no effect and tongues may fail, but the gift of divine dreams—these assuredly are the shadows of Divine Realities : I know many in this day who have been looking for them all their lives. I know also some who have found them ; but they could only be written in a Book of the Lesser Destinies by the help of a cipher alphabet. Ammonite is also a fossil.

Cat's Eye

I understand that this and its kindred are classed in the genus Agate, but I surrender to gem-specialists the things which concern their specialism and I claim for the *Book of Destiny* those which concern folk-lore, the old faiths and observances, the mystery of signs, omens and presages. Our stone was called in Assyria the Eye of Belus, and it was consecrated to that deity. It was held to carry felicity within its fair and speaking circles. The Cat's Eye has several sisters, as for example, the Lion's Eye and the Eye of

Adad, a god of Syria, but I do not know whether all can be identified at this day. It was efficient in respect of the terrors of the evil eye, and one speculates whether it was carried in secret by members of the papal household during the pontificate of *Pio Nono,* who was credited with this kind of affliction. In older days the Eye of Adad could save the sight of those who were attacked by small-pox, if the stone were passed occasionally over their eyes. Cat's Eyes are still supposed to impart health, riches and length of days. The Hindus say that Genii dwell therein.

Aqua Marina

The mythologists neglected this stone, having directed so much attention to the Emerald, with which it is in kinship by its colour. It should be worn by those who are in suffering, more especially if arising from sorrow. It is said to symbolise hope ; but these things notwithstanding, other fables connect it with inconstancy, for which reason it has been avoided by those who are betrothed.

Beryl

The reveries of later Kabalism have placed this rather morganatic or imputed sister of the Emerald under the presidency of the planet Jupiter, which imparts the gift of intelligence, as well as piety, modesty, fidelity and other characteristics that enter into the idea of generosity and virtue of soul. The Beryl is accordingly said to contribute its influence for the production of subtlety in spirit. It also promotes love between male and female, which indirectly is another quality of Jupiter, as the latter also presides over the propagation and preservation of the human species. The man who wears a Beryl will be likely to win by its aid the affections of the woman of his choice. In medicine it relieves sufferings which arise from liver and diaphragm. Once upon a time it was said that a fire could be kindled by exposing a Beryl to the sun's rays.

Chalcedony

is a mystic stone, a stone of the Holy City, a stone of priesthood. According to some Kabalists, it is under the dominion of the planet *Schabathai* or Saturn, which connects it with the transcendental sciences and the contemplation of Divine things. A variation of this is found in folk-lore tradition, which says that Chalcedony expels the phantoms of hallucination and gives victory over invisible powers which work for evil.

Coral

A stone which is not a stone, like the Philosopher's Stone in Alchemy. Coral has many virtues, and it is only in this century of disillusion that it is possible to recite them without seriously affecting the market prices. Because it preserved from misfortunes and maladies, the Romans wore it in their helmets; because it turned away the evil eye and aided dentition, Coral strings adorned the necks of their children. The *jettatura,* or evil eye, is still a terror to Italians and Coral amulets are still used to protect them; they are in the form of a minute hand extending the index and little finger only. Those who feel incited to murder may be turned from temptation by wearing Coral on their persons. It preserves from evil genii and from panics of fear; it is a safeguard for children against nocturnal terrors and for people generally against dreams in violent form. It confers reason and prudence; it calms tempests and stills the turmoil of the sea. It inspires gaiety, reassures the soul, cures complaints of the eyes and checks hemorrhage. Symbolically speaking, white Coral signifies modesty and the black variety means firmness and strength. The rosaries of catholic devotion are sometimes made therefrom, when the natural virtues — enhanced by priestly benediction—should form an efficient chaplet. The pilgrims to Mecca also carry chaplets and their beads are made of Coral.

Chrysoprase

In the planetary system of Kabalistic Magic, this stone is under solar influence and connects therefore with beauty, magnificence, science and all fortune. In the lore of the lapidary Chrysoprase is said simply to be a bearer of felicity. It has been pointed out, however, that a green variety of this stone belonged to the Duchesse d'Étampes, afterwards to Mary Stuart, Marie Antoinette and the Empress Eugénie—a long chaplet of misfortunes.

Cornelian

This is under the influence of Saturn, according to Kabalistic Science, and the testimonies concerning it offer wide and contradictory variations. Some say that it is not less admirable as a bearer of general felicity than it is rare, beautiful and precious. Those specimens which are red at the deepest are called symbols of joy and peace, expelling all sad and evil thoughts. The contrary testimony concerning the stone in general affirms that it induces fear, melancholy and mournful preoccupation of mind. But this being so, one of the commentators adds, it is admitted by all that it increases the flow of saliva in the mouth of babes. I suppose that even this virtue as a comforter of childhood has passed out of common knowledge.

Carbuncle

It would be strange if this gorgeous stone, wherein the richness and the glamour of the East seem concentrated into a single point, should not have been credited with signal properties in the seeing days of old, for which Nature was a world of symbols rather than of barren fact. Even at this day, he or she who can invoke with potent words, welling up from the heart's depths, shall find the Carbuncle answers with true oracles and yet with suggestions of greater things concealed in the dusk of its glorious deeps. The Kabalists seem right when they place it in the keeping of the sun, because it is an abyss of fire, and is in kinship with all magnificence and royal majesty. It was said of old to reflect the solar rays in obscurity and darkness, having previously condensed them in the light. In days nearer to these it was stated, on the authority of experiment, that if exposed to the sun's beams and allowed to absorb them, it would give them forth generously in the shadowed hours. I should not venture at this epoch of hard light to put the question to the proof, for when "all things bend and sink down in search of shameful pasturage," it may be that our want of faith has enfeebled the stones of price. I remember, however, with gladness that the Gates of the Mystic City are Gates of Carbuncles and that all its borders are of precious stones. For the Chaldæans it constituted a powerful natural talisman which drove away evil spirits and acted like a Rite of Purification, both on the moral and physical atmosphere. It preserves from incendiary, procures bright dreams, cures ophthalmic disorders and increases the vital heat. It symbolises ardour and the consuming fire of love. If this is on the physical plane there is a correspondence in things above, for the Carbuncle typifies also the rays of Divine Love, the radiance of faith and the impassioned zeal of charity. So is it true for those who are informed thereby that the Gates of the Mystic City are Gates of Carbuncle.

Crystal

Many things may pass as Crystal in the artificial terminology of glassware, but I speak here of the colourless hyaline quartz, to which alone the name belongs. Its ascribed virtues seem to arise in a very natural manner out of the impressions which it communicates externally to those who have sensibility of mind. It soothes and calms the senses, disposes towards sleep and induces good dreams therein. In symbolism it signifies transparency of soul and heart. Its more material virtues are to increase the milk of nursing mothers, relieve headache and elevate the emotions and mental faculties.

Diamond

I scarcely know why some of the Kabalistic school who practised Magic and studied—or perhaps dreamed concerning—the planetary influences, should have placed this, which is the gem *par excellence,* under the presidency of Mars. It is held, however, to be the chief symbol of love in the world of stones, and there is a certain lower sense in which Mars was a god of love, as well as of war. The Diamond signifies also innocence, constancy, fidelity, and, in the higher language of the virtues, it has been held to represent the absolute degrees of purity and strength. Its place among the precious stones mentioned in biblical records is sufficiently indicated by the fact that the High Priest Aaron wore a Diamond on his finger and divined thereby and therein. I do not know on what authority it is said that this stone turned black when the Jews sinned, crimsoned when they were deserving of death, but returned to its former colour in the presence of the innocent. Contemporary French occultism—which too often extends the circle of the secret sciences in the act of describing, and makes up legendary attributions as it goes—has discovered that the Diamond is the symbol of the sage who has stripped off all passion and lives in the absolute of complete intellectuality. There is authority in legend for the belief that it confers peace and serenity. When worn on the left side, it protects against enemies, paralysing their endeavours and bringing their snares to nothing. It has the same virtue in respect of wild animals and poisonous creatures. Because it renders those who wear it faithful to their engagements, there was a time when it adorned the wedding ring in Italian marriages, while on account of its virtue in love, the Diamond was held to secure the felicity of wedded pairs. Its sudden intervention—perchance as a gift—was thought certain to heal conjugal ruptures, and hence it was called the stone of reconciliation; but I regard the testimony as insufficient to constitute an inherent virtue—reconciliation by gifts having worked through many *media* from time immemorial. The list of its occult properties, powers and graces, might be continued indefinitely. In the psychic order of things, the Diamond induces somnambulism, dissolves enchantments, drives off were-wolves, as well as *incubi* and *succubi,* endows the understanding with lucidity, stills remorse—supposing that repentance has preceded—and in fine gives strength and courage. In the medical order, it purifies the blood, defends against epidemics, drives out poisons and prevents the ravages of insomnia. I will not criticise the alleged property of Diamonds to reproduce their species. I believe that this fable is reported by Boëthius and if verified might well claim to be regarded as an important item in his *Consolation of Philosophy.*

Emerald

Green is the great gift of beneficent and live Nature for the repose of the human eye amidst the blaze of sunlight and the splendour of the heaven. There is nothing in the world of precious stones so comparable to the rich verdure of meadows as the translucid Emerald. It is no wonder that many virtues are ascribed thereto. And, firstly, let me remind all—as they should know otherwise assuredly—that a great Emerald, graven with a Great and Sacred Name, adorned the Ephod of the High Priest in Jewry, and there was another among the gems of the Rational, as recorded in the Book of Exodus. It might be truly a symbol of life but legend connects it with immortality, by the hope of which life is fortified and maintained. It represents also inspiration and wisdom. Writers who are actuated by sentiment and poetic analogies, rather than by the lore of gems, have affirmed that the Emerald enlightens understanding, procures lucidity of spirit, eloquence and renown. It is said to deliver the possessed and to procure worldly fortune. On the physical side of health, it soothes the paroxysms of epilepsy, preserves from leprosy, softens the sufferings of childbirth and assists delivery. Finally, it strengthens sight and is like a tonic in extreme old age.

Garnet

There are many varieties of this stone, and the Carbuncle is said to be a Garnet exalted in the scale of magnificence. The virtues are many, like the species, for it signifies loyalty, frankness, lively faith, charity, constancy, friendship. It gives sincerity of heart. In the order of hygienic things, it purges vitiated air from pestilential vapours.

Hyacinth

I preserve or rather import this beautiful mythological name because of the gracious floral legend of which it reminds us. With us, in the common knowledge, it is a flower alone, but for the Latins it was a stone also and has passed from them to the French, who still use it to identify that which the Orientals term Corindon and which by us is known as Zircon, or Jacinth. The Kabalists place it under the rule of the Sun ; it represents the sun of thought and the divinity to which thought aspires. It is generous in all its varieties, like the solar heat and light; it procures terrestrial honours, health and the satisfaction of all desires for him who possesses and wears it. More important than these qualities, it signifies enthusiasm and poetry, which no doubt it was held to impart. In the lesser ways of its providence, the Hyacinth preserves from plague and poisons, from dangers on earth and sea, from storm and lightning. It induces sleep, fortifies and enlivens the heart of man.

Jade

In Japan and in China this is a sacred stone, and in the latter realm it was once, if not now indeed, regarded as a divine substance. The Hindus also held it in great esteem and singular veneration. In the East it is often a symbol of Divine Revelation, of grandeur, rectitude and immortality, and its name in Chinese is said to signify profound truth. In India, during other days, Jade could be possessed and worn only by men of great purity, whose passions were under complete control. There also it had many curative properties, and it is distinguished for these in the West. It has a powerful action on the renal system, relieves the pain of sciatica, cures epilepsy and poisonous bites. Finally, the Arabs say that it prevents bad dreams.

Jet

It is idle to class this substance among precious stones, save in respect of its virtues, which are many and signal; they are great in Magic and great also in Medicine. It is obviously a mourning adornment; its blackness has passed into a proverb; and it has come in this manner to symbolise grief, trouble and desolation of heart. But it gives victory over enemies, is a safeguard against all sorceries, expels spirits and phantoms. Like amber, it is of vegetable origin and burns freely, diffusing a certain odour—which used to be regarded as a potent disinfectant in epidemic diseases.

Lapis-Lazuli

According to the lore of the lapidaries, this stone is ascribed in a particular manner to the planet Venus; it symbolises and confers love; it represents also tenderness and simplicity of heart; it draws about those who carry it an atmosphere of gentleness and sympathy. It is also a stone of fidelity, while over and above these gifts it is excellent for the sight, enlivening to the spirits and soothing in feverish states.

Loadstone

This is the Herculean Stone of classical antiquity and Pliny includes it among gems, which is admissible on account of its most signal property, that of magnetic attraction. The Egyptians believed that it had great therapeutic virtues, and this notion was revived by Mesmer but relapsed speedily into oblivion. Still the legends of blessed Araby say (1) that if the eyelids are rubbed with Loadstone the love of the beloved is attracted; (2) that those who wear it experience a growth of understanding and will accomplish all their desires; (3) that it facilitates delivery; and (4) that if reduced to a powder and swallowed by those who have been poisoned, it acts as an antidote.

Malachite

is a type of tranquillity, is efficient in preventing litigation and brings success in business. It is one of the many symbols which represent hope.

Moonstone

It is pure as the queen of heaven, whose image is reflected into its name; it also makes for and maintains purity in those who wear it. It is a symbol of childhood, childlike nature and the clean heart in its openness. Even those who have grown old in the ways of the world, if they have not blotted out all early records of the heart, will find the Moonstone an evoker of enchanted memories—as it may be, of silver moons lighting the long past, of ever sacred nights, nights of innocent kisses exchanged in times of betrothal or in first days of espousal. It is a giver of conjugal felicity and to some also of prophecy. I have not heard of it in medicine, except as a safeguard from contagion.

Marcasite

As this mineral substance is susceptible of a fine polish, it is sometimes included in the lore of precious stones. It has no title by its nature or indeed by imputed virtue. It is merely a symbol of sadness.

Mother of Pearl

This also has no warrant for inclusion and I mention it only because it is usual to name it. There may have been occult qualities attached to it in the old days, because of its beauty, but I have met with no particulars.

Onyx

This is another stone which is in everlasting and pious remembrance because of its place in the pectoral of Aaron; but in the domain of folk-lore it is to be regarded askance on several counts. As a symbol, it signifies dole, discord, sadness and fear. It is held to occasion sleeplessness; it evokes phantoms and spectres, produces grievous dreams and stirs up quarrels. Against these ominous qualities it has two counter-balancing virtues; in things physical it arrests hemorrhage and in the moral order it renders the wearer chaste.

Opal

From the days of Pliny, the naturalists, the lapidaries, the poets have found the magic of the Opal put magic into their words concerning it. It possesses, in their descriptions, the fire of the carbuncle, the purple of amethyst, the brilliant green of emerald. It has concentrated the glories of morning; it is like a tear fallen from the moon; it is a rainbow veiled in white vapour; it is as stars of many colours shining in the Milky Way. But with all its beauty, it is a Stone of Destiny and that which it portends is ominous. It is fatal to love, or else the love which it procures is a consuming evil; at the best, from this point of view, it is the symbol of fickleness, variability and inconstancy of the heart and its affections. These opinions are, however, comparatively speaking, a recent growth of legend. In the days of Albertus Magnus, it was held not only to rejoice the heart of its owner but to make the heart amiable and beloved. Not only did it deserve to be called the Child of Love, but it gave beauty and wealth, was a buckler against misfortune, and he who carried it might even enjoy the gift of invisibility. The last quality has sometimes caused it to be regarded as the protector of thieves. Its most famous advantage was, however, that it turned pale in the presence of poison. Its lights also died out in the neighbourhood of its owner's enemy, while it blushed, as if with joy, when his friend was by. It was efficacious against contagion of the air, syncope, complaints of the heart and malignant diseases generally. When the bluish or milky tinge prevails in an Opal, it symbolises tears, prayers, pardon, and this kind increases fidelity.

Pearl

It may seem not a little incredible, but the *pretiosa margarita* is richer in the adornments of poetry than in those of legend; it seems even to have been neglected by the Kabalists, notwithstanding the pearls of Hagar. It has been held to be a symbol of faith, purity, and religious ardour. It softens violence and anger, gives patience and peace of soul. It is said to be a sign of tears, but I assume that they may be those of joy as much as those of sorrow. This is all that I can tell you concerning it.

Ruby

In the dusky deeps of this stone there is borne the burden of felicity. It is an emblem of beauty and elegance ; it banishes sadness and evil thoughts ; it restrains unlawful desire ; it soothes the troubled spirits ; it insures respect from all for those who wear it and smooths a way to the realisation of their lawful wishes. In the highest sense it symbolises charity, the fervour of Divine Love, as also loyalty, valiance. It will be seen in this manner that the felicity of which it is the bearer may be truly a sweet yoke and a light burden. But there is another side of the picture, for some accounts make its qualities depend upon those which belong to the wearer. Valour may be replaced by audacity and even impudence, loyalty by cruelty and the lust of blood, and charity by wrath in the degree that is deadly sin. No doubt its felicity is then changed into the heavy burden of guilt. Among its minor virtues is that it is a defence against lightning; moreover, it counteracts poison, quenches thirst, strengthens the heart and relieves headache. It gives warning of coming misfortune to the owner by changing its colour; and when fortune reigns again in his sky of destiny, it resumes its native hue. The Kabalists have assigned it to the sun.

Sapphire

It is under the influence of Saturn, according to the Jewish Magi; but these attributions vary in the different schools of symbolism; they are therefore subject to qualification and stand otherwise at their proper worth. It is of great scriptural importance, being the sixth stone on the Rational of Aaron, while tradition assures us that the Rod or Wand of Moses and the Tables of the Law were made of Sapphire. Here again the legend, like the attribution just mentioned, must stand at its value. As the Wand and Tables in question were used in offices transcending those of Nature, it is idle to object that Sapphires of such magnitude are found nowhere in the world. The story, however, may have a symbolical meaning. It is said that peace will encompass him who carries the stone on a pure and sincere heart; that it will defend him against the snares of the wicked and against consuming passions within his own fortress. It turns the heart to repentance and preserves the possessor from all evil. It is a lover of poverty—meaning no doubt the enlightened poorness or humility, nakedness and simplicity of those who are wise in God—wherein is a treasure of blessing. It symbolises justice, loyalty, beauty, nobility, truth and a pure conscience.

Topaz

This stone was allocated to the tribe of Simeon and appeared as such on the High Priest's Rational. Kabalism refers it to the Sun and all antiquity believed in its mysterious properties—as, for example, that it rendered the wearer invulnerable. This is on the authority of Heliodorus, in which case the mother of Achilles might have taken a simpler and better precaution than that of immersing her child in the River Styx. The Topaz has also a high place in Christian traditions, for it symbolises faith, justice, temperance, mildness, clemency, true love, disinterested friendship and love exalted to the Divine. There was never a stone which stood for so many and such signal virtues. In the worldly sense, it confers riches and honours; it inspires horror of blood, expels sadness and melancholy—like the anti-toxic virtue, a recurring office of stones—and preserves from sudden death, almost an unique quality. It is said also that it calms troubled waters, as if it were a talisman for the macrocosmic world, but perhaps this may be taken in the sense of stilling the waters of the human soul, because it is claimed otherwise that it appeases angry passions. Finally, as the Divining Rod is held to indicate the place of hidden springs and wells of water, so the Topaz is a Magnet for Gold, attracting the precious metal, indicating buried treasures and revealing lodes and veins of gold beneath the earth.

Turquoise

This is the Forget-me-not of the world of gems and is assuredly a perfect analogue or counterpart in stone of the gracious floral jewel. It does not seem to have any ancient history, whether legendary or otherwise, or at least outside of Russia, where it shares with the Topaz the virtue of insurance against violent death, including assassination, drowning and falls from heights. Arab nursing-mothers believe that it increases their milk. It gives the grace of activity, apparently in the physical order, and those who wear it can never fall into misery. It is strengthening to the eyes and a horse will not stumble which has a Turquoise placed in its hoof. The Arabs further say that it fills the human heart with hope and courage, that it insures love for its possessor, that it turns pale when disease befalls its owner and that it bursts, like a broken heart, when he dies. It is generally a symbol of youth, and the Persians find it efficacious if used as an amulet. It inspires young maidens with good and sincere thoughts.

Tourmaline

When exposed to the warmth of the fire or subjected to friction, this stone is said to become electric. It is said also that it polarises light. I have not heard that it has more occult qualities.

THE ALPHABET OF GEMS

As it is said that there is a destiny in names and as gems are used occasionally on bracelets to form the name of the beloved person to whom they are given, I do not feel that this trivial subject is entirely outside the somewhat elastic limits of a Book of Destiny. The alphabetical list which follows gives a few only out of many possible stones, less or more precious, and it shall be followed by an instance in point, to simplify still further a subject which in itself seems to be of uttermost simplicity and ease of practice.

A.—Agate, Amber, Amethyst, Aquamarine, Avanturine, the last being a species of feldspar.

B.—Beryl.

C.—Chalcedony, Chrysoberyl, Chrysolite, Chrysoprase, Coral, Cornelian.

D.—Diamond, Diorite—a name of Green-Stone.

E.—Emerald, Essonite—being a variety of Jacinth.

F.—Fluorine, *i.e.,* Fluor Spar.

G.—Garnet, Girasol, Green-Stone.

H.—Heliotrope, an alternative name of Blood - Stone; Hyacinth, alternative of Jacinth and Zircon.

I.—Iris.

J.—Jacinth, Jade, Jasper, Jet.

K.—Kokeul.

L.—Lapis-Lazuli.

M.—Malachite, Marcasite, Moon-Stone.

N.—The Niccolo, a form of Onyx.

O.—Onyx, Opal.

P.—Pearl, Peridot—a form of Chrysolite.

Q. — Quartz, many varieties of which, besides Rock-Crystal, are capable of polishing, but their names do not begin with this letter.

R.—Ruby.

S.—Sapphire, Sapphirine—a blue Chalcedony; Spath Adamantine, Spinel.

T.—Topaz, Tourmaline, Turquoise.

U.—Uranite.

W.—Water-Sapphire, a variety of Iolite.

Z.—Zircon.

It is obvious that the selection of stones to symbolise a particular name must be made with considerable care so that they may consort together, and as many letters are poorly represented, the matter must be often one of extreme difficulty. There are also letters to which no true stones are allocated. The Amethyst, Diamond and Aquamarine will answer for the name Ada; the Diamond, Onyx, Ruby and Amethyst represent that of Dora but will look curious enough as the letters stand in their sequence, while transposition seems somewhat opposed to the spirit of the device. In such cases and where a certain letter of a name, as in that of Zoe, has no stone to signify its presence, a little ingenuity in symbolism will overcome the difficulty by substituting a characteristic word representing the recipient of the gift in the eyes of the giver or the meaning attached to the name. For example, Dora signifies a gift and Theodora a gift from God, while the word gift is symbolised by Garnet, Iris, Fluorine, Topaz.

STONES OF THE TWELVE APOSTLES

St Peter—The Jasper.
St James—Chalcedony.
St John—Emerald.
St Matthew—Amethyst.
St Mark—Beryl.
St Simon—Sardius.
St Andrew—Sapphire.

St James the Less—Topaz.
St Philip—Sardonyx.
St Bartholomew—Jacinth.
St Thaddæus—Chrysoprase.
St Matthias—Chrysolite.

THE YEAR'S CHAPLET OF STONES

The months have their jewels like the planets and as the allocations vary among different nations, the birth Table which follows is without prejudice to any competitors that may be met with in magical calendars and the lore of gems. It is understood generally that neither man nor woman can err in choosing the stone of his birth-month to be worn in preference to others; it should have particular auspices of fortune on the natal day and throughout that month.

January—The Garnet and Zircon.

February—The Pearl, for which Slavonic traditions substitute the Amethyst.

March—Jasper, or according to the Slavs, Ruby.

April—The Diamond, or according to the Slavs, Sapphire.

May—Aquamarine.

June—The Agate, according to the Slavs.

July—The Ruby, according to the Latins: otherwise, Cornelian.

August—Moonstone, or Sardonyx.

September — Chrysolite according to the Slavs, but the Latins have substituted the Sapphire.

October—The Opal.

November—The Topaz.

December—Malachite according to the Slavs, and also Turquoise, which is the more general attribution. Chrysoprase is another alternative.

SIDELIGHTS ON WORKINGS OF DESTINY IN BUSINESS AND PLEASURE

OF FORTUNATE AND FATAL DAYS

I HAVE found it written in one of the gospels of commonplace expressed in paradox that business and pleasure are in reality but one affair, the explanation being that there are persons for whom pleasure is the business in chief of existence, while for others business is the palmary source of pleasure. Generalisations like this are meaningless, and I cite the particular specimen, firstly, because it happens to come from a pseudo-occult source, but, secondly, because it enables me to say that the traditions of old-world lore have recognised, amidst all natural and obvious distinctions, that there is one bond of union between work and play, occupation and enjoyment, which bond resides in the fact that there are days propitious for both and days also that are the reverse. In the microcosm it is a question of temperament characterising each personality ; in the macrocosm it is a question of sidereal influences acting upon different temperaments. Such influences are the results of planetary movements, and it is out of these movements that certain days have come to be regarded as felicitous in their effects on human beings, while certain others are baleful.

OF SHADOW AND LIGHT

Going back to the remote genesis of our race, it is an established fact that all customs which enter into the characteristics of a nation are results of observation and that the roots of many lie so far down that they must be sought in the very beginning of human knowledge. When science in the proper sense of the term had not yet entered into being, when human life was scarcely less simple than that of the beasts, it is to be inferred that human minds were not prone to speculation on the laws which rule the cosmos; but they were impressed assuredly by the succession of day and night, the rising and the setting of stars, above all by the splendid pageant of the sun's diurnal progress. The alternatives of darkness and light suggested the division of time into periods of days, the days were grouped into weeks, and these collected into months. It may well be that the deluge is a modern event, compared with this division.

In proportion as men advanced, a consciousness of the great cosmic laws grew within them, and these laws were connected more especially with those moving lights the life of which seemed most analogous to their own. To these stars they began also to attribute a direct and inevitable influence, presumably because observers had already imagined them as gods or the abodes of gods.

THE BAPTISM OF DAYS

The days of the week were partitioned among the moving lights, and the deities who ruled the planets prevailed in the days also : there was thus a certain harmony of government and kingship, both in heaven and on earth. It will serve no purpose here to enumerate the old names and connected allocations. After what manner the week was consecrated by Greece and Rome is familiar in the mouths of all. The kinds of influence exercised by Saturn, Mars, Venus and the rest of this week of gods are also known roughly and may be divined by children.

EVERY MAN HAS HIS DAY

Those whose birth took place under the predominant action of the sun, and during a conjunction favourable to the birth-moment, should initiate their serious affairs on Sunday. This does not mean that the day itself is propitious to action even in their case; it is not, in the manual sense. They should trace the great, general lines of the plan in view, either by thinking it out and leaving it to repose in the mind, or otherwise. When it is put into execution later on, under the influence of another day, there should be a success in the best sense.

I have mentioned a case about which there is no difficulty, that the hypothesis on which it depends may be quite clear to the mind. It must now be added that a pure planetary type is exceedingly rare in man; several stars impress their seals upon each individual being; and these astral signatures represent many influences, some of which oppose, some aid and some balance one another. The chief influences must be determined in the first instance and will give the directing line; secondary signatures may then receive attention; the planetary influences must be computed and a day chosen which seems propitious for a given action. For example, if the secondary influence acting upon an individual, who in the prominent sense is solar, should be Jupiter, it would follow that the undertaking which was planned on Sunday should be executed or begun on Thursday. This rule applies to all astral signatures.

It is therefore inexact to conclude that a

particular day is fatal, bad or unlucky; for some it may be highly fortunate, as would be the case with Friday for those whose natal star is Venus, for whom Venus is predominant in its influence, or even exercises an effect of an auxiliary kind. No days are unfortunate *per se,* though some are preferable to others for me and you. The Romans consecrated our Wednesday to Mercury and regarded it as ominous for Rome, because they were military rather than mercantile, whereas Mercury was a god of commerce and finance. On the other hand, the Phœnicians were a trading people, and the same deity, though he passed under another name, was one of their patrons.

THE DAY OF BATTLE

Other things being equal, it may be presumed that a battle fought on Tuesday, which is the day of Mars, will be a victory for that side on which the commander-in-chief belongs to the Martian type. A legion of volunteers should have notable success on this day, because those whose disposition is naturally towards military things are almost always Martian. It is likely to be otherwise with troops enrolled by conscription. But it must never be forgotten that victory is subordinate to that influence which prevails with the directing will, to the favourable circumstances which are seized by this will under that influence, and to the sudden lights flashing through the mind on the happy spur of the moment. For the rest, it is certain that he who is born to be painter, poet or musician will not shine as a leader of armies, that if a military career is somehow foisted upon him, it will not prove a path of lustre, and that if he shines at all therein it will be in discussing plans of campaign in the offices of the ministry of war rather than on the battle-field. The inspiration of the soldier comes from that influence which we have personified as Mars ; a born soldier is born under it ; others may be valiant through education, determination or utter necessity.

THE DAY OF LOVE

I am using the word somewhat in its conventional meaning ; that which at its highest rules all stars and systems is not in a governing sense under the influence of any ; people who are concerned therewith will not look for counsel from books dealing with destiny and above all the lesser fortunes. Such love is the destiny itself of all the worlds that are and of every world to come. The love which has its day is of another quality, another kind and degree. The influence which rules therein has been specialised under the name of Venus, and Friday is that day which is connected favourably with the affairs and offices of this power. Obviously, I do not mean that Friday will be always propitious to "affairs of the heart"; the Saturnian is likely to be scouted who goes to work therein; a son of Mars will do better, but not wisely and not always well; a Jupiter-subject will find his attraction degenerating into a banal flirt; and he who is of solar type will obtain an artistic satisfaction only. It will be far other than this for one who is under Lunar rule, and yet it will be transient even in his case. The Venusian only will find Friday full of lasting satisfaction for his love-undertakings.

Love of this kind is nothing, like the world to which it belongs, and I will turn therefore for a moment to the financial aspect of things. It is comparatively speaking rare to find the financial man marked with the seal of Jupiter; if he be so, let him avoid undertaking anything important on a Saturday, unless indeed it should have an agricultural aspect. His day of preparation, of planning and mental scheming should be Sunday, and he should act by preference on Wednesday.

NOTA BENE

Above all the hypotheses of occultism, above all the records of observation and experience on which they claim to be founded, there is the working of the Master of Worlds, Who alone rules in all. Man is no isolated being suspended in the vast creation, and all that is relative to him modifies for good or evil the primitive plan of his existence. The will with which he is endowed may intervene propitiously or otherwise in that which is called his destiny ; it may loosen or break the threads. Hence the importance of giving a straight and strong impulse thereto ; hence the need to temper it, so that it may resist all shocks. The man who can and does will, who wills with knowledge and power, is a motor for good or evil. Learn therefore to will, but will only that which is great and good, for otherwise we operate against the course and final end of the universe ; its law is greater than ourselves and it breaks those who are opposed.

SOME NAMES OF WOMANHOOD

THEIR MEANINGS AND ADORNMENTS IN COLOURS AND EMBLEMATIC FLOWERS

Name.	Origin.	Meaning.	Colour.	Mystic Flower.
Adelaide, Adela	German	Noble	White	Tuberose
Adrian	Greek	Of manly courage	Red	Dahlia
Agatha	Greek	Goodness	Blue	Heliotrope
Agnes	Greek	Chaste	White	Nenuphar
Albertina	German	Of high birth	Yellow	Camomile
Alexandrina	Greek	Guardian of warriors	Red	Amaryllis
Alice	German	Noble daughter	Golden Yellow	Buttercup
Alphonsa	Gothic	Ardent fire	Purple	Lobelia
Amanda	Latin	Worthy to be loved	Rose	Red Rose
Amelia	Visigoth	Powerful	Golden Yellow	Sun
Anastasia	Greek	One who raises up	Green	Absinthe
Angela, Angelica	Greek	Messenger	Purple	Aster
Anne, Anna, Annette, Nancy	Hebrew	Gracious above all	White	Jasmine
Antoinette	Etruscan	Daughter of Hercules	Green	Arum
Augusta	Latin	Sovereign	Gold	Camomile
Aurelia	Latin	Sun	Yellow	Helianthus
Beatrice	Latin	Happy	Blue	Borage
Bertha	German	Illustrious	White	Gardenia
Blanche	French	Pure	White	White Rose
Bridget	German	Procurer of safety	Yellow	Narcissus
Camilla, Camelia	Latin	Of free estate	White	Camelia
Caroline	German	Valiant	Bright Red	Pheasant's Eye
Catherine	Greek	Sincere	White	Pansy

Name.	Origin.	Meaning.	Colour.	Mystic Flower.
Cecilia	Latin	Sweet eyes	Blue	Myosotis
Celestina	Latin	Daughter of Heaven	Azure	Aster
Charlotte	German	Valiant	Bright Red	Louse-Wort
Clara, Clarissa	Latin	Remarkable	Yellow	Chrysanthemum
Claudia, Claudine	Latin	Chaste	Dark Blue	Pansy
Clementina	Latin	One who forgives	Violet	Scabious
Clotilda	German	Illustrious daughter	White	Lily
Constantia	Latin	Firmness	Blue	Iris
Cora, Coralie	Greek	Youth	Green	Reseda
Delphina	Greek	Fraternal	Blue	Ageratum
Dorothy	Greek	Gift of the gods	Purple	Peony
Eleanor	Greek	Fragrant	Flesh Tint	Blush Rose
Elizabeth, Isabella	Hebrew	God's pledge	Purple	Dahlia
Emily	Greek	Mild	Pale Blue	Blue-Bottle
Emma	Scandinavian	Protectress	Blue	Convolvulus
Ernestina	German	Serious	Yellow	Broom
Estella, Stella	Latin	Star	Blue	Aster
Esther	Hebrew	One who hides	Dark Blue	Pansy
Eugenia	Greek	Illustrious of birth	White	Hyssop
Eulalia	Greek	Well speaking	White	Clematis
Euphemia	Greek	High renown	White	Easter-Daisy
Euphrasia	Greek	Pleasure	Rose	Seringa
Felicia	Latin	Happy	Purple	Tulip
Fernanda	German	Amazonian	Bright Red	Cyclamen
Frances, Fanny	German	Hardy	Red	Eglantine
Gabrielle	Hebrew	Strength of God	Purple	Rhododendron
Genevieve	Celtic	Dweller in the woods	Dark Green	Arum
Gervaise	Greek	Respectable	White	Flax
Gilberta	German	Brave in peril	Scarlet	Azalea
Helen	Greek	Brightness of the sun	Golden Yellow	Helianthus
Henrietta	German	Worthy of honour	Yellow	Ebony-Tree
Honoria	Latin	Respected	White	Lily of the Valley
Hortensia	Latin	Lady of gardens	Blue	Hortensia
Irene	Greek	Pacific	Dark Green	Olive

Name.	Origin.	Meaning.	Colour.	Mystic Flower.
Jane	Hebrew	Full of grace	White	Acanthus
Josephine	Hebrew	Rich in gifts	Blue	Aconite
Julia	Greek	Adolescent	Green	Reseda
Justina	Latin	Equitable	Blue	Violet
Laura	Latin	Crowned	Green	Oleander
Leona	Greek	Brave as the lion	Scarlet	Amaranth
Louise	German	Celebrated	Golden Yellow	Angelica
Lucy	Latin	Luminous	Yellow	Calceolaria
Madeleine	Hebrew	Magnificent	Yellow	Margaret
Marcella	Latin	Martial	Red	Crocus
Margaret	Greek	Pearl	White	Margaret
Mary	Hebrew	Exalted	Rose	Rose
Martha	Hebrew	Provoking	Rose	Red Rose
Matilda	Hebrew	One who is given	Blue	Iris
Monica	Greek	Widow	Violet	Scabious
Natalie	Latin	Presiding over birth	Green	Reseda
Naomi	Hebrew	Splendour of beauty	Yellow	Gilliflower
Octavia	Latin	Eighth	Yellow	Marigold
Pamela	Greek	Queenly	Purple	Peony
Pauline	Greek	Small	White	Feathered Pink
Perpetua	Latin	Eternal	Purple	Immortelle
Philippina	Greek	Lover of horses	Red	Eglantine
Philomela	Greek	Lover of song	Green	Myrtle
Pulcherria	Latin	Most beautiful	Rose	Rose Nero
Rachel	Hebrew	Sheep	White	Honeysuckle
Regina	Latin	Queen	White	Lily
Rose, Rosina	Latin	Rose	Rose	Yellow Rose
Sabina	Greek	Pious	Blue	Lavender
Sarah	Hebrew	Princess	Purple	Geranium
Seraphina	Hebrew	Embraced	Purple	Tulip
Sidonia	Phœnician	Enchantress	Red	Anemone
Sylvia	Latin	Woodland born	Dark Green	Oak
Sophia	Greek	Wisdom	White	Convolvulus
Stephanie	Greek	Crowned	White	Lily
Susannah	Hebrew	Shining flower	White	Lily
Theodora	Greek	Gift of God	Purple	Lobelia
Theresa	Greek	Clever	Bright Red	Amaranth

Name.	Origin.	Meaning.	Colour.	Mystic Flower.
Ursula	Latin	Little bear	Grey	Flax
Valeria	Latin	Strong	Red	Valerian
Veronica	Greek	Image of the Saviour	Blue	Veronica
Victoria	Latin	Triumphant	Red	Laurel
Virginia	Latin	Virgin	White	Orange Blossom
Zepherina	Greek	Bearer of life	Green	Arum
Zoe	Greek	Life	Yellow	Chrysanthemum

CURIOSITIES OF PLANETARY LORE

THE HEPTAMERON OF PLANETS AND OF DAYS

THE Doctrine of the Magi recognised seven principal planets, the influence of which is manifested more especially and directly on animals and inanimate Nature here below. In the order of their distance from earth, these are: Saturn, Jupiter, Mars, Venus, Mercury, with the two greater luminaries, the Sun and Moon, regarded as the generators of life.

They recognised also that the celestial sphere is divided by the number 12, and they separated in like manner the hours of the day and night. They attributed further a planet to each hour and to each day of the week, and by means of the planetary symbol of the Heptagram they indicated the moving lights and the days which succeed one another.

In this star of seven rays the planets are placed according to the enumeration given above, proceeding from Saturn to Jupiter and so onward, the Sun and Moon intervening.

That which is called the order of the Hermetic Hierarchy proceeds from Saturn to Luna and so onward, in a reverse order, through the angles of the Heptagram. There is finally

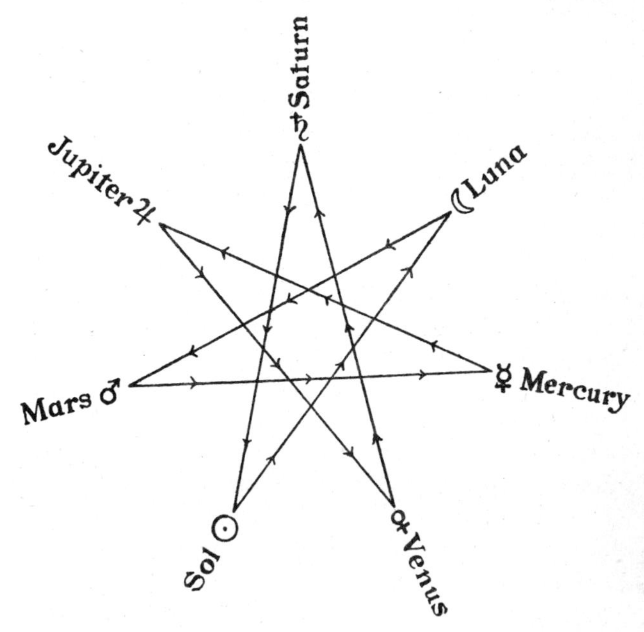

a distinct progression beginning with the Sun and indicated on the lines of the figure by means of arrow-heads. This progression gives the days of the week in their order with the planets attributed to each. It can scarcely be necessary to enumerate, but the succession is as follows: Sunday = the Sun; Monday = the Moon; Tuesday = Mars; Wednesday =

Mercury; Thursday = Jupiter; Friday = Venus; Saturday = Saturn.

The hours of each day are distributed under the planetary influence after the ensuing manner.

Sunday

Hours of the Day: 1st Hour (counting from Midnight), the Sun; 2nd Hour, Venus; 3rd Hour, Mercury; 4th Hour, the Moon; 5th Hour, Saturn; 6th Hour, Jupiter; 7th Hour, Mars; 8th Hour, the Sun; 9th Hour, Venus; 10th Hour, Mercury; 11th Hour, the Moon; 12th Hour, Saturn.

Hours of the Night: 1st Hour, Jupiter; 2nd Hour, Mars; 3rd Hour, the Sun; 4th Hour, Venus; 5th Hour, Mercury; 6th Hour, the Moon; 7th Hour, Saturn; 8th Hour, Jupiter; 9th Hour, Mars; 10th Hour, the Sun; 11th Hour, Venus; 12th Hour, Mercury.

Monday

Hours of the Day: 1st Hour, the Moon; 2nd Hour, Saturn; 3rd Hour, Jupiter; 4th Hour, Mars; 5th Hour, the Sun; 6th Hour, Venus; 7th Hour, Mercury; 8th Hour, the Moon; 9th Hour, Saturn; 10th Hour, Jupiter; 11th Hour, Mars; 12th Hour, the Sun.

Hours of the Night: 1st Hour, Venus; 2nd Hour, Mercury; 3rd Hour, the Moon; 4th

Hour, Saturn ; 5th Hour, Jupiter ; 6th Hour, Mars ; 7th Hour, the Sun ; 8th Hour, Venus ; 9th Hour, Mercury ; 10th Hour, the Moon ; 11th Hour, Saturn ; 12th Hour, Jupiter.

Tuesday

Hours of the Day: 1st Hour, Mars ; 2nd Hour, the Sun ; 3rd Hour, Venus ; 4th Hour, Mercury ; 5th Hour, the Moon ; 6th Hour, Saturn ; 7th Hour, Jupiter ; 8th Hour, Mars ; 9th Hour, the Sun ; 10th Hour, Venus ; 11th Hour, Mercury ; 12th Hour, the Moon.

Hours of the Night: 1st Hour, Saturn ; 2nd Hour, Jupiter ; 3rd Hour, Mars ; 4th Hour, the Sun ; 5th Hour, Venus ; 6th Hour, Mercury ; 7th Hour, the Moon ; 8th Hour, Saturn ; 9th Hour, Jupiter ; 10th Hour, Mars ; 11th Hour, the Sun ; 12th Hour, Venus.

Wednesday

Hours of the Day: 1st Hour, Mercury ; 2nd Hour, the Moon ; 3rd Hour, Saturn ; 4th Hour, Jupiter ; 5th Hour, Mars ; 6th Hour, the Sun ; 7th Hour, Venus ; 8th Hour, Mercury ; 9th Hour, the Moon ; 10th Hour, Saturn ; 11th Hour, Jupiter ; 12th Hour, Mars.

Hours of the Night: 1st Hour, the Sun ; 2nd Hour, Venus ; 3rd Hour, Mercury ; 4th Hour, the Moon ; 5th Hour, Saturn ; 6th Hour, Jupiter ; 7th Hour, Mars ; 8th Hour, the Sun ; 9th Hour, Venus ; 10th Hour, Mercury ; 11th Hour, the Moon ; 12th Hour, Saturn.

Thursday

Hours of the Day: 1st Hour, Jupiter; 2nd Hour, Mars; 3rd Hour, the Sun; 4th Hour, Venus; 5th Hour, Mercury; 6th Hour, the Moon; 7th Hour, Saturn; 8th Hour, Jupiter; 9th Hour, Mars; 10th Hour, the Sun; 11th Hour, Venus; 12th Hour, Mercury.

Hours of the Night: 1st Hour, the Moon; 2nd Hour, Saturn; 3rd Hour, Jupiter; 4th Hour, Mars; 5th Hour, the Sun; 6th Hour, Venus; 7th Hour, Mercury; 8th Hour, the Moon; 9th Hour, Saturn; 10th Hour, Jupiter; 11th Hour, Mars; 12th Hour, the Sun.

Friday

Hours of the Day: 1st Hour, Venus; 2nd Hour, Mercury; 3rd Hour, the Moon; 4th Hour, Saturn; 5th Hour, Jupiter; 6th Hour, Mars; 7th Hour, the Sun; 8th Hour, Venus; 9th Hour, Mercury; 10th Hour, the Moon; 11th Hour, Saturn; 12th Hour, Jupiter.

Hours of the Night: 1st Hour, Mars; 2nd Hour, the Sun; 3rd Hour, Venus; 4th Hour, Mercury; 5th Hour, the Moon; 6th Hour, Saturn; 7th Hour, Jupiter; 8th Hour, Mars; 9th Hour, the Sun; 10th Hour, Venus; 11th Hour, Mercury; 12th Hour, the Moon.

Saturday

Hours of the Day: 1st Hour, Saturn; 2nd Hour, Jupiter; 3rd Hour, Mars; 4th Hour, the Sun; 5th Hour, Venus; 6th Hour, Mercury; 7th Hour, the Moon; 8th Hour, Saturn; 9th Hour, Jupiter; 10th Hour, Mars; 11th Hour, the Sun; 12th Hour, Venus.

Hours of the Night: 1st Hour, Mercury; 2nd Hour, the Moon; 3rd Hour, Saturn; 4th Hour, Jupiter; 5th Hour, Mars; 6th Hour, the Sun; 7th Hour, Venus; 8th Hour, Mercury; 9th Hour, the Moon; 10th Hour, Saturn; 11th Hour, Jupiter; 12th Hour, Mars.

The Magi have also allocated the 12 Signs of the Zodiac to the 12 Hours of the Day and Night as follows: ARIES governs from 12 midnight and from noon to 1 o'clock; TAURUS from 1 to 2; GEMINI from 2 to 3; CANCER from 3 to 4; LEO from 4 to 5; VIRGO from 5 to 6; LIBRA from 6 to 7; SCORPIO from 7 to 8; SAGITTARIUS from 8 to 9; CAPRICORNUS from 9 to 10; AQUARIUS from 10 to 11; PISCES from 11 to 12.

Later Astrology has postulated that the first Zodiacal Hour must begin with the sign governing the month, as follows: The Sun is in the Sign of ARIES from March 20 to April 18. During this period the first hour of the day and night must begin with ARIES and the 12th hour will then complete the circle of the Signs with PISCES, as in the tabulation above. The Sun is in the Sign of TAURUS from April 19 to May 18; the first hour of the day and night is therefore referred to TAURUS, while, following this order, the 12th hour will be referable to ARIES. From May 19 to June 17 the 1st Hour will be in correspondence with GEMINI and the 12th with TAURUS. The succession continues thus: June 18 to July 17, 1st Hour=CANCER; 12th Hour=GEMINI. July 18 to August 16, 1st Hour=LEO; 12th Hour=CANCER. August 17 to September 15, 1st Hour=VIRGO; 12th Hour=LEO. September 16 to October 15, 1st Hour=LIBRA; 12th Hour=VIRGO. October 16 to November 14, 1st Hour=SCORPIO; 12th Hour=LIBRA. November 15 to December 14, 1st Hour=SAGITTARIUS; 12th Hour = SCORPIO. December 15 to January 13, 1st Hour=CAPRICORNUS; 12th Hour=SAGITTARIUS. January 14 to February 12, 1st Hour=AQUARIUS; 12th Hour=CAPRICORNUS. February 13 to March 14, 1st Hour=PISCES; 12th Hour=AQUARIUS.

PLANETS AND SYMBOLS OF THE ELEMENTS

The elements of old-world lore are represented by equilateral triangles. That of Fire is a simple figure, having the apex upward, thus:

It answers to the East and the season of Spring-tide. The zodiacal correspondences are ARIES, which is the Sign of Fire; LEO, the Sign of Growth; and SAGITTARIUS, the Sign of the End. The Sun is the ruling chief during the Day Hours, and to him Jupiter is subject. In the Night Hours this order is reversed, Jupiter predominating and the Sun ranking as second. The planet Saturn divides the empire with both.

The triangle of Air has the apex upward, but is intersected by a horizontal line, thus:

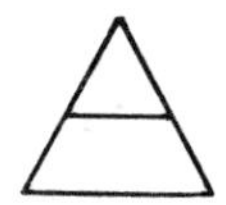

It answers to the South and the season of Summer. The zodiacal correspondences are GEMINI, from which Air derives its principle; LIBRA, which is the Growth thereof; while the End is AQUARIUS. Saturn dominates the Day and Mercury is subject thereto. In the Night this order is reversed. Jupiter divides the empire with these planets.

The triangle of Water is a simple figure, having the apex downward, thus:

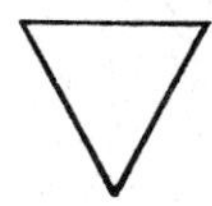

It answers to the West and the season of Autumn. The zodiacal correspondences are

CANCER, which is the principle of Water; SCORPIO, which is the increase thereof; and PISCES, which is the end. Venus rules the Day and Mars is subject thereto. In the Night this order is reversed. The Moon divides the empire with these planets.

The triangle of Earth has the apex downward, but is intersected by a horizontal line, thus:

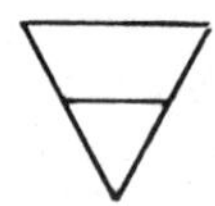

It answers to the North and the season of Winter. The zodiacal correspondences are TAURUS, which is the principle of Earth; VIRGO, which is the Growth thereof; and CAPRICORNUS, which is the End. Venus rules the Day, and the Moon is subject thereto. In the Night this order is reversed. Mars divides the empire with these planets.

BIRDS, BEASTS, AND FISHES CONSECRATED TO THE PLANETS

SATURN governs among (a) *Birds:* Pewet, Raven, Owl; (b) *Beasts:* Ass, Mole, Camel, Wolf and Serpent; (c) *Fishes:* Eel.

JUPITER governs among (a) *Birds:* The Eagle, Peacock and Pelican; (b) *Beasts:* The Elephant, Stag and Lamb; (c) *Fishes:* The Dolphin.

MARS governs among (a) *Birds:* The Vulture, Falcon and Hawk; (b) *Beasts:* The Wolf, Leopard and Hyena; (c) *Fishes:* The Barbel and Pike.

SUN governs among (a) *Birds:* The Phœnix, Swan and Cock; (b) *Beasts:* The Cynocephalus, Lion, Ram and Horse; (c) *Fishes:* The Sea-Horse.

VENUS governs among (a) *Birds:* The Dove, Turtle and Swallow; (b) *Beasts:* The Goat, Calf, Bull and Rabbit; (c) *Fishes:* The Tithymal.

MERCURY governs among (a) *Birds:* The Stork, Parrot and Magpie; (b) *Beasts:* The Dog, Hare, Fox and Monkey; (c) *Fishes:* The Mullet and Trochus.

MOON governs among (a) *Birds:* The Goose, Duck and Diver; (b) *Beasts:* The Chameleon, Panther, Hind and Cat; (c) *Fishes:* The Crab.

TREES AND PLANTS CONSECRATED TO THE PLANETS

WITH AN ACCOUNT OF THEIR MEDICINAL VIRTUES, UNDER PLANETARY INFLUENCE, ACCORDING TO OLD HERBALISM

A.—Under the Presidency of Saturn

I.—*Narcotics and Toxics:* Aconite, Hellebore, Monkshood, Hemlock, Opium, Poppy, Solanum.

II.—*Leprosy, Obstructions of the Bladder, Diseases of the Spleen, and Dental Maladies:* Pine, Cypress, Tamarind, Yew, Henbane, Savine.

III.—*Dysentery, Hemorrhage and Hemorrhoids:* Taboul, Asphodel, Hemp-seed, Agnus-castus, Mandragore, Burdock, Fern.

IV.—*Miscellaneous Diseases:* (a) *For Phthisis and Quartan Fever*—Polypody; (b) *For Stone and Gravel*—Hart's-tongue; (c) *To expel Stone*—Saxifrage; (d) *To promote the Growth of Hair*—Philophthelela.

V.—*Other Plants and Trees:* The Fig, Parsley, House-leek, Cumin, Rue, Benzoin.

B.—Under the Presidency of Jupiter

I.—Balsam, *for outward wounds and inward lesions;* Betony, *for obstructions of organs and internal ulcers;* Flax, *for ulcerous wounds and decline;* Red and White Currant-Tree, *for affections of the throat, liver-complaint and heat of the stomach;* Persicary, *a sovereign remedy for gout and an excellent dressing for wounds;* Tenerion, *for pestilential fevers;* Mullen, or lung-wort, *for wounds and hemorrhage.*

II.—*Other Plants and Trees:* Bugloss, Agrimony, Mace, Ears of Wheat, Mastic, Mint, Inula, Darnel, Poplar, Oak, Ash, Hazel, Pear, Apple, Vine, Plum.

C.—Under the Presidency of Mars

I.—Lesser Esular, *for dropsy, to soften and remove hard skin, corns, etc.;* Rest-Harrow, *for pleurisy and obstruction of the bowels;* Thistle, *for decline, pleurisy, dysentery and other morbid fluxes;* Nettle, *for tumours, asthma, pleurisy and gouty humours:* Armogloss, *for violent headache.*

II.—*Other Plants and Trees:* Garlic, Eschalot, Onion, Spurge, Leek, Radish, Mustard, Scammony, Plantain, Small Laurel, Dogberry, Cypress.

D.—Under the Presidency of the Sun

I.—Marigold, *for the eyes and inflammation generally;* Immortelle and Tamarind, *for fluxions, epilepsy, apoplectic seizures, chills, and as a tonic for the brain;* Ash, *as a tonic for the heart and for poisonous bites;* Balm-Mint, *as a tonic in old age, also for liver and lungs;* St John's Wort, *for internal and external wounds;* Enula, when infused in wine, *to strengthen the sight and cure asthma;* Laurel Leaves, *for poisonous bites;* Citron, *as a prophylactic;* for which purpose the pips should be steeped in wine.

II.—*Other Plants and Trees:* Turnsol, Peony, Celidony, Ginger, Gentian, Dittany, Ivy, Mint, Lavender, Marjory, Rosemary, Aloes, Meadow-Saffron, Clove, Pepper, Palm, Cedar, with all trees and plants which give forth odoriferous gums, like Musk, Benzoin, Mastic and Storax.

E.—Under the Presidency of Venus

I.—Rose, *for uterine and connected affections;* Nenuphar, *for vertigo, consumption, pleurisy and liver-complaints;* Lily, *for childbirth, deafness, falling sickness, paralysis;* Pisterion, *the root of which cures ulcers and stops hemorrhage.*

II.—*Other Plants and Trees:* Vervain, Violet, Maidenhair, Orange, Valerian, Thyme, Coriander, Sandal, Myrtle and Box.

F.—Under the Presidency of Mercury

I.—Hazel-Tree, *the essence of the wood being held excellent for the sight when the Moon is in conjunction with Mercury;* Sweet Marjory, *for nervous complaints, great lethargy in sleep and apoplexy;* Cubeba, *to strengthen memory;* Anise, *for obstructions;* Snakewood and Moneywort, *for asthma;* Juniper, *for dropsy and colic;* Trefoil, *for epilepsy;* Daisy, *for mouth and tongue, also for fluxions;* Beans, *for gravel and stone, if roasted, ground and infused like coffee-berries;* Camomile, *for colic and ulcerated lungs;* Cinquefoil, *the root of which heals wounds, the juice reduces swellings of the glands, and the leaves stop toothache.*

II.—*Other Plants and Trees:* Fumitory, Pimpernel, Smallage, Cinnamon, Cassia, Mace.

G.—Under the Presidency of the Moon

I.—Melon, *for fevers and inflammation of the stomach;* Colewort, *for bile;* Garlic, Onion and Leek, *for the brain;* Poppy—the double variety—mixed with oil of Juniper—*as a brain tonic;* Mandragora, *for epilepsy and melancholy;* Linden or Lime-Tree, the water of which, distilled when the Moon is in the Sign of Pisces, is good for *complaints of the stomach;* Mushrooms, *for dropsy;* Peony, *to regulate the blood.*

II.—*Other Plants and Trees:* Moonwort, Palm, Hyssop, Agnus Castus.

COLOURS CONSECRATED TO THE PLANETS

The old Magian Philosophy recognised three primary colours as resulting from the decomposition of light: they were blue, red and yellow. The intermediate colours are formed by the combination of two primaries. Red and yellow produce orange; blue and red make violet; green is formed by the admixture of blue and yellow. White is not a colour, but is light in its perfect state; it is the same with black, which is darkness and the emblem of chaos. Saturn is in correspondence with black; Jupiter with azure; Mars with red or crimson; the Sun is yellow or golden; green and rose are attributed to Venus; Mercury answers to a blending of colours, like opal; the Moon answers to white.

Colours are symbols and the sense of these

symbols is in correspondence with the powers, virtues, or qualities ascribed to the planets. Yellow is the symbol of riches because it is the colour of gold, and in a broader sense the generous gold of sunshine is the wealth of all the world. Red, as the colour of blood, is the emblem of force and valour, in correspondence with Mars. Jupiter is a planet of religion, and blue—which is heaven's own tincture—is the emblem of faith. Green is the colour of renewal, the token of hope, and is rightly attributed to Venus, because the planet of birth is the planet also of regeneration, or the second birth of man. This indication belongs to the Greater Mysteries. But the alternative colour of Venus is rose, recalling the mystic flower which bears this gracious name ; it is the emblem of love, which is another name of Venus ; it is the bond between heaven and earth, the ladder of ascension and the gift to the life of man as a title of entrance to that which is the life of life. Saturn represents mystery—and death, which is one aspect of mystery. The colour in analogy with these is black ; it is emblematic of the sorrow of our mortality ; but it signifies also renewal, the transformation of life, because it is through the night of the tomb that we enter into the glory of resurrection. Mercury is in correspondence with the suffusion or radiance of many colours ; it is the messenger or bearer of tidings in planetary symbols and reflects from the Word of Life, wherein are the Graces of the Spirit, as seven qualities of lustre. White is the emblem of purity, and the Moon is a vestal-virgin even in motherhood.

HIGHER ASPECTS OF PLANETARY COLOURS

1. Saturn = Black. The negation of colours, which is represented by darkness, not only symbolises impenetrable mystery in the absolute sense, but the silence imposed on those who are initiated into the Mysteries and have entered the secret path of transcendental science. It is the keeping of the secret in the heart, lest the Word of Life be wasted.

2. JUPITER = Blue. This colour is in analogy with all things to which the azure sky is referable itself in symbolism. It represents therefore the heaven of our spiritual desire, the soul, faith, the assurance into which faith passes, the help which comes from on high, the reward which God has prepared for those who love Him, the forms of worship belonging to external religion. In another order of things it signifies understanding, intellectual supremacy, friendship and, in a sense, justice.

3. MARS = Red. This colour is in analogy with all things to which Mars is

referable by the exaltation of its vulgar attributes. The God of war and victory shadows forth other struggles and other conquests than those of material battles. There are the struggles of the soul in its reaching out towards Divine ends; there is the valour which is not of this world; there is that which overcomes all things. Mars is also love in one of its aspects, and this is true on all the planes, because love is a warfare on all of them, till peace is signed in attainment.

4. The SUN = Yellow, Orange; and these colours signify the splendours of the mind as well as material riches, the honours that are above as well as those conferred below, realisation, fruitfulness, experience, and the Divine degrees thereof.

5. VENUS = Green. The three theological virtues of Faith, Hope and Charity are all in a sense represented by the colour ascribed to Venus. It is assurance, reliance, confidence, expectation, the eye looking forward and upward. Venus herself is Love, and together they testify to peace, sensibility, remembrance, renovation, the youth of the spirit and the world to come.

6. MERCURY = Purple, Opal. The former colour is emblematic of Divinity, supreme power, pontifical religion, science, beauty, glory, art and poetry.

7. The MOON = White, but especially in

the fair shining and splendour thereof. White is not only purity, innocence, chastity, virginity ; it is also truth, the mystery of the soul, the soul in its beauty—as a reflection of the Eternal Sun.

It is right to add that there are lower aspects of planetary colours, but of these it is unnecessary to speak more than in passing. BLACK may indicate hypocrisy, falsehood, treason ; RED may represent passion in its grossness ; YELLOW has analogies with distrust and jealousy ; even virgin WHITE may be the colour of sterility, weakness and indifference.

THE WHEEL OF WISDOM

AT the beginning of the old manuscript from which I have derived this process, it is said that it shall be attempted only by those whose faith in God has become to them as the substance of knowledge, after which it proceeds, in another manner of language, to give account of the Seven Spirits or Intelligences set over the Seven Planets, with all that is attributed to these and is placed under their influence among animate and inanimate things, according to the occult understanding concerning the order of the world. The diagram of the Wheel of Wisdom is placed as a frontispiece to the present volume, and therein will be found the names, signs and attributes belonging to each planet. It may be mentioned that they follow a scheme of distribution which in certain points and respects may be called peculiar to itself.

The Intelligence of Saturn is ORIPHIEL, who in the common sense of Magic presides over building operations, agriculture and metallurgical pursuits. Now, Saturn is the Greater Infortune according to astrological doctrine and its Intelligence has operation in events which are connected with sickness, death and sorrow. These are, however, on the side of the planet in its severity, but on the side of grace there are intellect, deep thought and the great patience of stars. ORIPHIEL has rule in these, and above him is the Unknown Power which for those who are on the path of wisdom so orders all things that they shall not miss the goal. He governs those Mystic Houses which are not built with hands; those hidden fields of consciousness and life into which some who are called may enter, to sow and to reap therein; those mysteries of sanctity and adeptship wherein is communicated the experience of mystic death. He who aspires to such experience and shall make himself properly prepared in all parts of his nature shall be under the providence of this Great Spirit as his warden, and when he invokes him there shall be a sure answer.

The Intelligence of Jupiter is ZACHARIEL, who presides over happiness, health, riches and greatness of soul. But these are on the natural side, and above him there is another Great Spirit who presides over spiritual felicity, the health of our higher being, the wealth of the knowledge of God and the ineffable greatness of His attainment. He who aspires to eternal joys rather than those that are temporal shall prepare himself to this end, shall abide under the tutelage of the Spirit who rules in these and the Spirit will respond to his call.

Mars is the Lesser Infortune and the Intelligence of this planet is SAMAEL, who presides over war, discord, destruction and violent death. But this is on the side of severity, while on that which belongs to grace there are valour, nobility and the strength called invincible. Above SAMAEL there is a third Great Spirit in the hiddenness, who takes these qualities and uplifts them, so that they become valiance in the conquests of adeptship, nobility in divine desire and invincible strength of soul in the glorious work of God.

The Intelligence of the Sun is MICHAEL; power, victory and glory are in the hands of him; but above him is the Great Spirit by whom is communicated the power which saves the soul, the victory of adeptship and the glory of the saint exalted among the celestial thrones. Lift up your eyes, O Aspirant, and behold the King in his beauty.

Venus is the planet of love, and its Intelligence, who is ANAEL, governs the relations of the sexes, as well as all grace, beauty and joy in the natural order of things. Above these natural humanities there is the Great Spirit who is the channel of Divine Love in its descent from heaven to earth and in its ascent from earth to heaven. Earth and heaven are united in communion with this Spirit; and if thou, O Student of the Stars, shalt seek him with a clean heart and a zealous mind, thou shalt know the secret correspondence between things above and below and the inner meaning of that Hermetic doctrine which establishes similitude between them.

The Intelligence of Mercury is RAPHAEL, who in the natural order of the planet is held to administer both good and evil, quickness of thought and speech, science and the means of its attainment, the material wealth which comes to those who are ready of hand and head. But wit may descend to the unworthy tricks of sharpness, the craftsman's skill into craftiness and riches may be obtained by fraud. Leave therefore the pairs of these alternatives and cleave to the Great Spirit who rules in the transcendence of Mercury, for with and in him there is that which is desired by the wise. He shall teach thee, O Seeker for the Masterhood, in what region abides the Divine Science and how we may attain its treasures.

The Moon is governed by GABRIEL and he rules in things of the imagination, as well as in lesser ways of human life and mood. Above him is the seventh Great Spirit, by whom the world of images is dissolved in the real light, the light which can enlighten every man who cometh into this world. Leave therefore the shadows of the mind and look for the true day.

It is said in the old book that the animate and inanimate things, the times, seasons and numbers ascribed to the planet in the Diagram are like degrees by which we may ascend from the lowest to the highest. I can testify to the truth of this, because all Nature is sacramental. He who has entered the path of the Mystic Marriage under the auspices of the Great Spirit who abides in Venus, when Venus is exalted in God, shall know the mysteries of the No. 6, which is the triad in its duplication, and why Christ was crucified on the day referred to Venus. He shall know the symbolism of the Emissary Goat which was sent forth to be devoured in the wilderness. Plant and bird and beast, fish, mineral and stone will unfold before him as symbols, and each symbol will carry a message to his heart.

If I sought to unfold such meanings in their fulness this section would be itself a book; but I mean it only as a suggestive indication to a small minority of readers who even in a collection of old-world lore are expecting to find some gate which for them will open on the infinite. For their benefit I add one other word. The Seven Great Spirits are within you; the lesser intelligences are also within, with their good and evil aspects; all the planetary attributions are facets of your own nature ; and the Diagram is your own personality projected on a certain plane. Remember therefore the Divine Names in the middle of the Wheel of Wisdom and realise their relation with your centre. This is Secret Doctrine indeed ; but I am giving you the only Key to the Wheel and true directions for its use in the operations of Higher Magia.

THE LITTLE BOOK OF DIVINATION BY FLOWERS

IN ACCORDANCE WITH HERMETIC DOCTRINE CONCERNING SOLAR AND LUNAR INFLUENCES

THE MODE OF DIVINATION

THERE is a time-honoured feeling concerning the Language of Flowers ; but the little handbooks which circulated in earlier days are merely inventions of phantasy, and if they have any significance, it is owing to surface analogies of an exceedingly obvious kind. Outside these there are the legends and the old customs connected with the floral calendar ; properly the latter belong to folklore and are important after their own manner within the measures of that science. I believe that the methods of floral divination are many, but they also are purely artificial in character. It will come as a surprise to the studious that there is, outside these, an art of the subject which is put forward with serious claims. Very little is known regarding it, and the practice so far has passed into expression after rather an involved manner. It is worth while to disentangle it, so that those who are drawn into this unrecognised by-way of botany may have the facts and the practice before them in a concise form.

The hypothesis from which it depends is that the floral world, taken as a whole, is placed directly under the sun's influence, the proof being that under this influence they pass through all their stages from bud to blossom. At the same time there are certain flowers which confess to the moon's government, being those which bloom at night; but this notwithstanding, their formation and growth are the work of the star of day. It is necessary therefore to know in the first place the nature and quality of solar and lunar influence. In respect of the former, there is no need to say that flowers are produced at all seasons of the year, the winter period included, though they are then far less abundant. It follows that the influence on vegetation varies with the period of the year. That plant which blossoms when the sun is in its ascendant receives a different influence from that which is exercised at the opposite time of year. In other words, the nature of the solar influence varies with the distance of the great orb from the earth. The influence is further subject to the action of stellar radiation, which is equivalent to saying that it is governed by the sun's position in the Houses of the sun—otherwise, the Zodiacal Signs. Hereunto must be added the effect of the moon, when the plant is subject thereto, and in general astrological sense. The true and fundamental method of divination by flowers is based on these considerations and the procedure may be formulated thus.

Select that flower which is intended to furnish the oracle ; let it be done on a day favourable to the designed question and in a mental condition properly disposed thereto. It must be the day also on which the flower in question is in a state of perfect bloom. Combine the presages furnished by the sun according to that Sign through which it is then passing, and those of the moon according to its age in the calendar. This combination will furnish the requisite answer. Before proceeding further, two divinatory examples may be given to clear the issues. Let it be assumed that the question is one of marriage. The flower which is the matter of the oracle must be chosen on a Friday, this being the day of Venus. We will assume that it is in full bloom on May 21—when the sun is in the Sign of Gemini—and on the 9th day of the moon, as shewn in any almanac. The combination of presages will then give an answer as follows :

Moderate fortune : Coming discord. This is equivalent to saying that the expected marriage will not take place, being hindered by disagreement. As the Sign Gemini further presages the recurrence of a previous event, there is ground for inferring that the approaching rupture will be a repetition of one which has taken place previously, or alternatively, that it will be followed by a similar breach destined to occur later on.

If the proposed question concerns a business matter, the flower chosen for the oracle must be in full bloom on a Wednesday—let us say, June 30, the sun being in Cancer and the moon at the full. The answer will be then as follows : Prosperity and favourable chances, but unstable result, want of permanence, notwithstanding the prospect of money.

To follow these examples intelligently it is only necessary to study the *Table of Solar Influences on the Twelve Signs* and the *Table of Lunar Powers.* The flower itself will have been chosen in accordance with the indications of the *Lexicon,* and its time of blossoming will be ascertained from the section entitled *The Season of Blooms.* The *Lexicon* can be also used independently for message-purposes, and a number of flowers collected into a bunch or bouquet may convey the purport which would otherwise be contained in a letter of considerable length. Flowers seen or gathered by chance may serve as oracles.

SYMBOLISM OF COLOUR IN FLOWERS

The colour which reigns exclusively or is dominant in each flower is one of its chief forms of expression, a prime element of its language, and the meaning attributed thereto is in strict analogy with the scheme of planetary colours, for the Doctrine of the Magi, in its root-matter, is the essence of the harmony which prevails through the whole creation. Unfortunately, it is only its fragments that we meet with—for the most part — in books. The rainbow of floral colours is interpreted as follows:

WHITE signifies: Innocence, Virginity, Candour, Purity of Heart. In this it corresponds with the Moon, which, as I have said, is a Vestal Virgin.

RED signifies: Modesty, the blush of Sacred Shame, so long and unintelligently regarded as a sign of guilt. On the rare occasions when this ascription happens to be correct, it is a witness to the shame of guilt, as a fire kindled in the conscience and suffusing the face. Floral Red is a symbol also of Love and its holy Ardour. In the sense of lower desire it may signify Sensuality and Luxury. It is in planetary correspondence with the force and valour of Mars, for true love has the strength and courage of Galahad.

YELLOW signifies: Generosity, Wealth, Fertility and Plenty on all planes. In the sense of its affliction it may announce conjugal misfortune. It is in analogy with the wealth of the Sun.

BLUE signifies: Elevation of Soul, Piety, Refined Feeling, Wisdom. Blue is the colour of Jupiter, and it will be remembered that this is a planet of religion.

BLACK signifies: Dole, Tears and Death. It is attributed also to Saturn, wherein is the Great Mystery. But there are no really black flowers, just as there is no death, and herein lies the force of the symbolism.

PURPLE signifies: Great Ambition, Power, High Estate. These things have also their higher side; as such, they belong to the Red of Mars in combination with the Blue of Jupiter.

ROSE signifies: Youth, Elegance, Tender Love, and for obvious reasons arising from these meanings, it is one of the colours of Venus.

GREEN signifies: Hope, Growth, Life, and it is the other colour of Venus.

A SHORT LEXICON OF THE LANGUAGE OF FLOWERS

APRICOT—Hope frustrated—*e.g.*, unrequited love.

ABSINTHE—Bitter sorrow, regret, reproach.

ACACIA (White)—Pure love.
ACANTHUS—Modesty.
ACONITE—Protection.
AGAPANTHUS—Pleasure, delight, rapture.
AGNUS CASTUS—A precious treasure.
ALMOND—Mildness; sometimes deception.
ALOES—Quarrel, strife, acerbity.
AMARANTH—Tireless devotion.
AMETHYST—Gift of pleasing.
ANDROMEDA—Combat.
ANEMONE — Desolation, abandonment, sometimes perseverance.
ANGELICA — Ecstasy of delight, purest thought.
ANISEED—Great sweetness, pledge given.
APPLE-BLOSSOM—Fortune.
ARUM—Aspiration, soul of feeling.
ASTER—Thoughts of love.
ASTRAGAL—Regret.
AURICULA—Seduction.
AZALEA—Happiness.

BALM-MINT—Strength of soul.
BALSAM—Petulance, impatience.
BASIL—Wretchedness, disdain.
BEGONIA—Coldness.
BELLA-DONNA—Coquetry.
BETONY—Friendship.
BLACKBERRY-FLOWER—Envy.
BLOODWORT—Tenderness.
BLUE-BELL—Fidelity.

BORAGE — Bluntness, sometimes mildness.

BUTTER - CUP — Mockery, sometimes riches.

BOX—Piety.

BROOM—Slight hope, demand.

CALCEOLARIUS—Marriage.

CALYCANTHUS—Hope.

CASTUS—Oddness, strangeness.

CAMELIA—Constant love, love's felicity.

CAMOMILE—Submission.

CAMPANULA—Coquetry.

CARNATION—Kisses.

CATCH-FLY—Tender affection.

CENTAURY—Felicity.

CHERRY-BLOSSOM—Careful education.

CELANDINE—Affection.

CHESTNUT—Defence, pleading.

CHICORY, WILD—Frugality.

CHRYSANTHEMUM—Forlorn hope.

CINERARY—Suffering.

CITRON—Promise of a letter.

CLEMATIS—Coquetry, also devotion.

COBŒA—Intimacy.

COLOCYNTH—Bitterness.

COLUMBINE—Gaiety.

CONVOLVULUS—Separation, absence.

CORN-POPPY—Calm.

CORONILLA—The heart's wealth.

COWSLIP—Youth.

CUCKOO-PINT—Delay.

COCK'S COMB—Impatience.
COW-WHEAT—Tenderness.
CROCUS—Sentiments.
CYCLAMEN—Jealousy.
CYPRESS—Dole.

DAHLIA—False abundance.
DANDELION—A fair future.
DAPHNE—Amorous curiosity.
DIGITALIS—Labour—delay.
DITTANY—Gratitude.
DOG'S TOOTH—Great troubles.

EASTER-DAISY—Heart-yearnings.
EBONY-TREE—Severe virtue, also impatience.
EGLANTINE—Poetry, love.
ELDER-FLOWER — Beneficent moroseness.
EUPHORBIA—Love.

FENNEL—Sweetness, promise given.
FEVER-FEW—Fruit of love.
FIG-TREE—Great sweetness.
FERN—Domestic felicity.
FLAX—Protector.
FRAXINELLA—Gratitude.
FRITILLARY—Admiration.
FUCHSIA—Tender adoration, amiability.

GARDENIA—Homage.
GENTIAN—Bitterness.

GERANIUM — Affection, tenderness, caprice.

GILLIFLOWER—Amiable simplicity, constancy.

GOLDEN-ROD—Great joy.

GOOSEBERRY—Joy.

GLADIOLA—Assignation.

GOLDY-LOCKS—Joy.

HELIOTROPE—Tenderness, sometimes—love betrayed.

HAWTHORN—Prudence.

HAZEL-TREE—Pardon.

HELLEBORE—Cultivated mind.

HEATHER—Solitude.

HEMP—Useful toil.

HEMLOCK—Courage, also treason.

HOUND'S TONGUE—Endurance.

HOLLYHOCK—Simplicity.

HONEY-FLOWER—Sweetness.

HOUSE-LEEK—Coldness.

HORTENSIA—Uncertainty.

HYACINTH—Tears, fidelity.

HYSSOP—Mystery of the heart.

IMMORTELLE—Immortality.

IRIS—Hope, tender love.

IVY—Attachment.

IXIA—Lasting love.

JASMIN—Love's dawn, love's delight.

JONQUIL—Languor.

LARKSPUR — Carelessness, thoughtlessness.

LAUREL—Honours.

LAVENDER—Mystery, respect.

LEAD-WORT—Tenderness.

LILAC—Love, especially first love.

LILY—Purity, majesty.

LILY OF THE VALLEY—Beauty.

LOBELIA—Love.

LUCERN—Health.

LYCHNIS—Resignation.

MAGNOLIA—Great generosity.

MANCHINEEL—Deception.

MAPLE—Wisdom, strength.

MAIDEN-HAIR—Discretion.

MALLOW—Sweetness, sorrow.

MEADOW-SAFFRON — Ill-nature, jealousy.

MARSHMALLOW—Charitable spirit.

MELILOT—Sweetness.

MISTLETOE—Evil knowledge.

MARGUERITE—Love.

MARIGOLD—Solitude, jealousy, sadness.

MARJORAM—Beauty, consolation.

MINT—Memory.

MIGNONETTE—Kisses, modest mien, hope of love.

MIL-FOIL—Valiance.

MIMOSA—Love.

MONKEY-FLOWER—Love.

MOONWORT—Indiscretion.

MULLEN—Delay.
MULBERRY—Prudence.
MYOSOTIS—Remembrance.
MYRTLE—Protection, confession.

NETTLE—Wickedness.
NARCISSUS—Pride, coldness.
NASTURTIUM—Heart aflame.

OLEANDER—Lasting glory.
OLIVE—Peace.
ORANGE-BLOSSOM—Virginal purity.
ORCHIS—Faith.

PALMA CHRISTI—Children.
PANSY—Think of me.
PARIETARY—Vexation.
PARSLEY—Repast.
PASSION-FLOWER—Suffering.
PATCHOULI—Worldly.
PEACH—Felicity, heart's rapture.
PEAR—Betrothals.
PELARGONIUM—Feasting.
PEONY—Regrets, homage.
POPPY—Sleep, dreams.
PERIWINKLE — Sight, lively remembrance.
PETUNIA—A letter intercepted, also—meanness.
PHLOX—Flame of love.
PLANTAIN—Poverty.
POMEGRANATE—Folly, passion.

PRIMROSE—Youth, first love.
PLUM-BLOSSOM—Independence.

RANUNCULUS—Perfidy.
RASPBERRY BLOOM—Fine speech.
RHODODENDRON—Abundance, pride.
ROSE—Treasures of beauty and grace.
ROSEMARY—Agreeable presence.
RYE-GRASS—Work and fortune.

SAINFOIN—Heart's emotion.
SALICARIA—Respectful ardour.
SAW-WORT—Affection.
SAXIFRAGE—Disdain.
SCABIOUS—Consolation.
SCILLA—Coldness.
SEAL OF SOLOMON—Protestation.
SENSITIVE PLANT—Shame.
SERINGA—Beauty, confession.
SNAPDRAGON—Desires.
SNOWDROP—Hope.
SOAPWORT—Regrets, great qualities.
SUNFLOWER—Gratitude, dazzlement.
SPIRÆA—Mystery.
STRAWBERRY PLANT—Urbanity.
STAR OF BETHLEHEM—Purity.
SWEET WILLIAM—Kisses.
ST JOHN'S WORT—Attempt, siege.

THISTLE—Stubborn misanthropy.
THORN-APPLE—Disquietude.
THYME—Activity.

TREFOIL—Doubt.

TUBEROSE—Voluptuous love, admiration.

TULIP — Confession — grandeur, declaration.

TOBACCO-PLANT—An obstacle removed.

VALERIAN—Heart's wound, also ease of access.

VANILLA—Compliments.

VERONICA—Fidelity, attachment.

VERVAIN — Enchantment, also — confidences.

VIOLET—Modesty.

WATER-LILY—Coldness.

WATER-GLADIOLE—Hour of meeting.

WORM-GRASS—Return.

YEW—Tears.

YUCCA—Concealed ardour.

ZINNIA—Inconstancy.

THE SEASON OF BLOOMS

I have distributed this part of the subject under the Twelve Houses of the Sun, which is the name given by astrology to the Twelve Zodiacal Signs. The flowers and plants classified in the list which follows are those which usually put forth their blossoms during the periods represented by the Signs. Allowance must be made, however, for variations of climate in different places and in the same places during different years. Natural growth is assumed in any case and not greenhouse culture.

I

Aries

The Sun traverses this Sign between March 20 and April 18. It is the Season of Bloom for the following Flowers and Plants.

Cowslip	Aniseed
Anemone	Moonwort
Arum	Seal of Solomon
Bugloss	Scilla
Fritillary	Chrysanthemum
Bloodwort	Tree Peony
Marigold	Coronilla
Cherry	

II

Taurus

The Sun traverses this Sign between April 19 and May 19. It is the Season of Bloom for the following Flowers and Plants.

Cyclamen	Columbine
Gladiola	Asphodel
Gentian	Gooseberry
Ixia	Geranium
Snapdragon	Daisy
Peony	Honey-Flower
Saxifrage	Lily of the Valley

Azalea	Narcissus
Calycanthus	Almond
Honeysuckle	Laurel
Lilac	Mignonette

III

Gemini

The Sun traverses this Sign between May 20 and June 20. It is the Season of Bloom for the following Flowers and Plants.

Aconite	Amaranth
Clove	Amethyst
Flax	Astragal
Mullen	Campanula
Phlox	Hound's Tongue
Valerian	Lily
Ranunculus	Lychnis
Lavender	Poppy
Seringa	Catchfly
Orange	Oleander
	Blackberry

IV

Cancer

The Sun traverses this Sign between June 21 and July 21. It is the Season of Bloom for the following Flowers and Plants.

Agapanthus	Basil
Aster	Betony
Chrysanthemum	Nasturtium

Dahlia	Balm-Mint
Fraxinella	Carnation
Spiræa	Sainfoin
Pomegranate	Scabious
Myrtle	Fuchsia
Hortensia	Andromeda

V

Leo

The Sun traverses this Sign between July 22 and August 22. It is the Season of Bloom for the following Flowers and Plants.

Milfoil	Dahlia
Balsam	Immortelle
Cactus	Lobelia
Centaury	Monkey-Flower
Digitalis	Golden-Rod
Melilot	Clematis
Sunflower	Heliotrope
Veronica	Yucca
Jasmin	

VI

Virgo

The Sun traverses this Sign between August 23 and September 21. It is the Season of Bloom for the following Flowers and Plants.

Meadow-Saffron	Bella-Donna
Tobacco-Plant	Goldy-Locks
Vervain	

VII

Libra

The Sun traverses this Sign between September 22 and October 22. It is the Season of Bloom for the following Flowers and Plants.

Meadow-Saffron	Zinnia
Narcissus	Chrysanthemum

When the sun is passing through Scorpio, Sagittarius and Capricornus, between October 23 and January 18, the flowers are few and far between, while none of them seem to contribute to the language of the subject. At the year's beginning, under the Sign of Aquarius, or between January 19 and February 17, we are concerned only with Hellebore, Primrose, Cowslip, Crocus, the early Iris ; and under the Sign of Pisces, or between February 18 and March 19, with Easter Daisy, Tulip, Snowdrop, Blue-Bell, Gilliflower, early Mignonette, Daphne. The reader will understand that I have cited only those flowers and plants which possess meanings in the language.

A TABLE OF SOLAR INFLUENCES IN THE TWELVE SIGNS

Our next consideration is the diversified power and influence exercised by the Sun in each of the zodiacal signs.

ARIES.—The Sun foretells advancement in all walks of life, though possibly after some vicissitudes or alternations. Specific enterprises are characterised by weakness.

TAURUS.—The Sun foretells disputes, quarrels, actions at law. Whatsoever is acquired under this Sign has the seal of permanence.

GEMINI.—The Sun predicts tolerable chances only. There is danger of loss, either in goods or money. Fraud is indicated. Something which has happened before will recur under this Sign.

CANCER.—The Sun brings tidings of favourable chances and prosperity. Some tribulations may be expected. The events which take place under this Sign are wanting in permanence.

LEO.—The Sun indicates happy chances, gains, rise of fortune and stability.

VIRGO.—The Sun testifies concerning difficulty in undertakings, impotence, travels to come. There will also be sudden recurrence towards a resolution taken previously.

LIBRA.—The Sun prophesies adversity,

obstacles, change in resolve and weakness in results attained.

SCORPIO.—The Sun gives favourable chances and protection, but there is warning of illness to come. There is permanence in that which is brought to pass under this Sign.

SAGITTARIUS.—The Sun gives presage of happy chances; but there are many preoccupations, struggles and passions at work.

CAPRICORNUS.—The Sun is like a pledge proffered to success in enterprise, but the outlook is unfavourable to love. Things which occur under this Sign are destined to change and pass.

AQUARIUS. — The Sun prognosticates success, chances to come and stability in results acquired. But enmities have to be reckoned with.

PISCES.—The Sun has only moderate chances to offer and there is also the play of passions. There will be either the recurrence of an event which has come to pass previously, or a new event will be repeated later on.

THE WEEK OF FLOWERS

We have seen in *The Mode of Divination* that a flower must be chosen on Friday for a question concerning Marriage and on Wednesday for a question of business interest. It follows that there is a Floral Week, and this again is in strict correspondence with the sphere of influence governed by each planet. It must not be overlooked in the attempt to understand correctly the secret speech of flowers. Choose therefore the blossom which is in occult correspondence with the question on which you seek information ; and choose it also on the day to which the question belongs, according to the planetary scheme.

A.—You shall choose it on a SUNDAY if it be a matter of money, for the Sun is gold.

B.—Make your choice on a MONDAY, if it be a question of health.

C.—The influence of Mars is exercised over all manners of strife and struggle, as over warfare in the ordinary sense. Choose your flower on TUESDAY if your inquiry be concerning any matter in dispute, any legal case or thing under discussion.

D.—But if it be a business question, an interest of this kind, or one of benefit, healing or travelling, make your choice on WEDNESDAY.

E.—The day of Jupiter is THURSDAY, and then shall your flower be selected, if the case in point be of a religious kind or one of general probabilities.

F.—Choose, however, on FRIDAY in matters of love, marriage and divorce, for Venus rules in these.

G.—Saturn is a House of Mystery, and all questions of higher interest, all mysteries belong thereto. Choose your flower on a SATURDAY, if you are dealing in matters like these.

A TABLE OF LUNAR POWERS AND INFLUENCES

The day of the New Moon, first quarter, Full Moon and last quarter will be found in every almanac; it is therefore easy to calculate the moon's age on any day of the lunar month. In the following table the paragraph numbered 0 represents the birth of the New Moon, that numbered 1 answers to the succeeding 24 hours, and so forward to the 15th day, which is that of the Full Moon, thence to the 29th day, this being the eve or vigil preceding the next New Moon.

0.—NEW MOON. Welcome and profitable friendships, end of preoccupations and fatigues.

1.—Downfall of an enemy. Journeys. Long illness. Discord.

2.—Reconciliation. Chance in a journey. Short illness. Chance in money.

3.—Good fortune. Dangerous illness. Undertake nothing. Chance in sea-voyage.

4.—Enmity. Vengeance. Good to begin an enterprise. Dangerous for illness.

5.—Favour or protection. Fatal for illness begun on this day. Good for health.

An illness to come shortly will end on this day.

6.—Benevolence. Forecast favourable for love. Undertakings begun on this day will be fortunate.

7.—Acquisition. Illness begun on this day will be of brief duration. Forecast favourable for marriage.

8.—Victory. Fortunate for journey begun. Forecast bad for illness.

9.—Dangerous for beginning of an illness. Good for voyages and travels. Discord at hand.

10.—Fortunate for undertakings. Diseases begun may end fatally. Aid against an enemy.

11.—Good for travelling. A dangerous woman. Favourable for money-matters. News at hand.

12.—Rupture of friendship. Poor chance. Bad for illness. Favourable for sea-voyages.

13.—A day of marriage. Mischance. Dangerous for illness. Good for travelling.

14.—Separation. Chance. A sickness begun on this day will prove mild. Bad for travel by land.

15.—FULL MOON. New friendship. Sickness will be slight. Chance in money. Do not travel.

16.—Good for money-matters. Forecast unfavourable for marriage. A journey indicated.

17.—Presage of something prejudicial. Mischance in undertakings. Chance in money.

18.—Presage of illness. Discord. Vengeance. Do not travel. Bad news.

19.—Good for health. Presage of a child. Bad for travelling.

20.—Presage of illness. Good for enterprises. Losses in money.

21.—Recuperation. News of illness. Good for travelling. Favourable chance for personal interests.

22.—Avoid all undertakings. Dangerous for the beginning of sickness. A cure may take place. News by letter. Money.

23.—Chance for a favour. An illness begun may prove a long one. Separation. Cure at hand in some complaints.

24.—An illness begun may prove a long one. News near to the heart. Good for money. News by letter.

25.—Vengeance. Favourable to personal interests. Dangerous for illness. Bad in matters of love.

26.—Favourable to pleasures. Serious for illness. Presage of union. Good for personal interests.

27.—Good for enterprises. A sickness begun on this day will prove variable. Favourable for personal interests. Bad for travelling.

28.—An illness begun on this day will prove

slight. Favourable for undertakings. Marriage. Good for personal concerns. News of money.

29.—Bad inspiration. Unfortunate news. Sickness. Long expected news may come.

THE MYSTERY OF DREAMS

OF DREAM AND VISION

I SUPPOSE that the popular occult hypothesis concerning dreams is that they are infused or otherwise occasioned in the soul of man for his instruction and warning. It is a part of this hypothesis that the interpretation of dreams can furnish revelations of our destiny, like some other forgotten sciences. As regards the interpretation itself, there are neither general nor particular laws, but there is a very large body of meanings or explained cases which cover most of the experiences obtained in sleep; and these meanings are, also by the hypothesis, a result of ancient observation which has come down to our days. So far as there is a philosophy of the subject—though it does not deserve to be dignified by this name—it has nothing to do with occultism and it does not draw from tradition. Chaldeans, Assyrians, Greeks and Romans believed in the importance of dreams and sought to explain their meaning. The rough and general thesis, or recognised root-fact, was formulated by Hippocrates, who says that when the body is asleep, the spirit maintains its vigil, proceeds at will wheresoever the body can go and beholds all that the physical eyes can discern in the waking state. I leave out of consideration all questions of higher conditions, in virtue of which it was supposed that certain gifted souls could transcend the normal sphere of vision and enter into hidden worlds. These possibilities are beyond all popular tradition and do not enter into the interpretation of dreams. They involve the idea that truth and not picture-symbols was revealed to the seer.

There are four kinds of dream, to which different names are given, according to the quality of each: the first is simple dream, the second vision, the third reverie, while the fourth is called apparition. In simple dream the truth is held to be manifested under certain symbolic images; it is a kind of picture-writing or pageant enacted within the psychic nature of the dreaming man, but sometimes in such a manner that he is actor-in-chief. As an instance of the simplest kind, Pharaoh beheld a group of seven fat kine and then another group consisting of seven lean beasts, but it was Joseph who gave him the meaning. Septimus Severus succeeded Pertinax after dreaming that he had taken possession of the horse which threw the emperor mentioned. Queen

Hecuba, with child of the notorious Paris, brought forth in dream a firebrand which consumed the city of Troy. Astyage, King of Medea, saw his daughter give birth to a vinestalk, and in due course he became the grandfather of illustrious Cyrus. The Queen of Macedonia dreamed that she was stamped on the breast with a seal representing a lion, and this took place when she was bearing the great Alexander within her. Amilcar was warned in his sleep that he would sup on the morrow in a beleagured city, and he entered one as a fact, but it was in the guise of a prisoner of war. The stories of this kind are endless.

The usual characteristic of vision is that it takes place in the waking state, and at its highest it may be that which is understood as Divine Revelation. A simple instance, apart from any message, is when Jacob was met by the angels of God at the place which he called Mahanaim. There are also visions of the night which are distinguished by their importance from dreams, but the distinction is somewhat arbitrary. The three Magi were warned in this manner not to return to Herod ; the angel commanded Joseph to take the young child and his mother and flee into Egypt ; the ladder which was shewn in his sleep to Jacob is classed as a vision rather than a dream. On the other hand, prophetic experiences like those of Isaiah represent vision in the absolute sense of the word and are apart from experiences in slumber, whether these are great or small.

Reverie, as it is commonly understood, is synonymous with the state of brown study, or intense preoccupation; as such, it is without consequence and calls for no interpretation. There is, however, an arbitrary use of the term which is found in a few works on the interpretation of dreams; it is concerned with the repetition in sleep of strong impressions present to the mind during the waking hours. That which has been thought —and deeply in most cases—in the day is dreamed during the night. Persons who are afraid of certain unwelcome encounters are apt to dream that they have actually occurred. So also he who is always brooding over money will have it with him in his sleep, and a substantial supper in the evening may reappear as a banquet at night.

I am following an old classification without pretending to sustain its especial merits. The use of the term apparition to distinguish a fourth aspect of dreaming seems to identify the state with that of hallucination, because such apparitions are said to be seen by those who are decrepit and weak in mind, or else by young children. Veridic apparitions would belong to the order of visions. The reader will be likely to dispose rather summarily of a tabulation which will have little to his purpose, and he will be satisfied to regard dreams as things heard, seen and acted in sleep, while visions, as intimated already, are experiences in the vigil of waking life.

In respect of dreams, it has been laid down by interpreters that those which are only remembered in part are useless for explanatory purposes; that those which occur immediately after retirement are not to be trusted, because the process of digestion is still at work in the organism; and that those which belong to the break of day are those which may enter into the realm of seership.

There are further two chief kinds of dreams, as dreams are understood by the classification already made. The first kind is called speculative or contemplative. A case in point is that of the prisoner who dreamed that he was about to be hanged and that the rope was already round his neck, when one who stood near drew his sword and set him free. This was realised next day, for he was condemned to death and was already in the executioner's hands, but was rescued by armed men employed by his friends for the purpose. The second kind is called allegorical or speculative and their fulfilment is never of the literal and actual class. The communication is by way of enigma and symbol. To see a serpent in dream portends enemies and ingratitude; an appearance like that of an angel is understood to mean revelation. That which is signified does not as a rule come to pass for at least several days. It is to be remarked that only persons of pure life, temperate habit, clear understanding and sound judgment are likely to have important dreams; excesses, in eating or drinking especially, tend to cloud the bond of kinship which subsists between the present and future. The dreamer's physical and other conditions must therefore be known, or must be gauged approximately, before his experiences in sleep can be translated for his own or for our instruction. The gift of interpretation, moreover, is a gift of seership; it is not possessed by many and at its highest is a faculty confined to few indeed. I should not recommend my readers to attempt it on their own part, especially in the case of others, as the guidance usually involved by reading in the *Book of the Sleep of Life* is not without its responsibilities. It may happen that in our own experience we enter into the sphere of Dream-Symbolism and a light may come to us regarding that which is signified. It should be observed and checked with care, for it may be the sign of an awaking gift. Its development is possible only in life on the path of adeptship, and adeptship is a synonym of sanctity. For the ordinary man and woman, taken even at the best and highest, there is no other course open but to study the records of the past, and some extracts from the findings are, for this reason, provided in the present place.

TABLE OF THE DAYS OF THE MOON FOR THE INTERPRETATION OF DREAMS AND VISIONS

The first day of the Moon is that of the New Moon, when the Moon is new in the morning. But when the New Moon arrives in one of the evening hours, the first day is counted from the morning after. The lunar month has sometimes 29 days and sometimes 30, including of course that period during which it abides in the hiddenness.

First Day of the Moon: Dreams are fortunate.

Second Day: That which you have dreamed has no truth in it.

Third Day: Dream is without consequence.

Fourth Day: Dreams are fortunate, and you may look for their fulfilment.

Fifth Day: They are entirely futile, and nothing can follow therefrom.

Sixth Day: Be very careful, and see that you tell your dream to nobody.

Seventh Day: Keep your dream in mind, because there is truth in it.

Eighth Day: Something will follow from your dreaming: it has a purpose.

Ninth Day: You will see a result at once.

Tenth Day: It will be true and will come to pass with joy.

Eleventh Day: The realisation will be with you in four days.

Twelfth Day: You will have cause to remember your dream, because it will be realised by its opposite.

Thirteenth Day: That which you dream will be true, and there is no question concerning it.

Fourteenth Day: It will happen, but long after.

Fifteenth Day: The realisation will be with you in thirty days.

Sixteenth Day: That which you have dreamed will come to pass.

Seventeenth Day: Tell no one till the third day thereafter.

Eighteenth Day: Be careful; the dream is likely to be made void.

Nineteenth Day: Keep it in your mind: you will have joy in the heart because of it.

Twentieth Day: You will assuredly see the result; and that in four days' time.

Twenty-first Day: Put no trust therein, for nothing will come of it.

Twenty-second Day: Be patient for a few days only, and you shall see what you shall see.

Twenty-third Day: The dream will be fulfilled in three days.

Twenty-fourth Day: It will bring you much satisfaction.

Twenty-fifth Day: It will come to pass in eight or nine days.

Twenty-sixth Day: Take heed: this is important for you.

Twenty-seventh Day: Great contentment will follow hereon.

Twenty-eighth Day: It is true and will come to pass with joy.

Twenty-ninth Day: Rest assured — the dream is true.

Thirtieth Day: It will come to pass on the same morning.

SYMBOLISM OF THE FOUR ELEMENTS IN THE WORLD OF DREAM

A.—The Presages of Fire

1. Those who are accustomed to see fire in their sleep are prompt and choleric in their temperament. The dream of fire is usually an aftermath of anger, to which the person so troubled has been subject the day previously.

2. To be scorched in dream signifies an attack of slight fever.

3. To see a slow fire, without sparks or smoke, argues perfect health; sometimes an abundance of good things; and sometimes a feast or other rejoicing in the company of relatives and friends.

4. A great fire, full of sparks and smoke, foretells unwelcome news or quarrels of a minor kind.

5. To see fire extinguished means poverty, want, bad fortune ; but in the case of a sick person, it means speedy cure.

6. A lighted candle or lantern, burning brightly, promises restoration to health, supposing that the dreamer is ill. It is also a sign of marriage for single persons, and generally of success in undertakings.

7. A lantern or candle burning in a dull manner, or extinguished, forebodes sadness or sickness, but neither will last long.

8. To dream that one is in a ship and watching a far-off light burning clearly means that no wind will trouble us and that we shall come into port safely. This may refer to enterprises as well as voyaging.

9. It is a good sign to dream that one is holding a lighted torch. In the case of young people, they will be fortunate in love, will attain their end, overcome their enemies and be honoured and welcomed by everyone.

10. To dream that another person is holding a lighted torch signifies that the evil which we have done will be discovered and that requital will follow.

11. An extinguished torch has the opposite meaning in each of the above cases.

12. To see a house burning with a clear, silent, unconsuming fire means possessions

for those who are destitute, riches and inheritance. Those who are rich already will have honours conferred upon them, whether in the way of charges, dignities, or otherwise.

13. But if the fire is violent, crackling, and if the house seems about to be consumed, the opposite of these is portended.

14. When a man dreams that his bed is burning, this threatens damage, sickness, or unpleasantness for his wife. The significance is the same for a woman.

15. The burning of household goods, involving their destruction in this manner, means damage or contrariety for the master of the house.

16. The burning of the lady's boudoir, or the larder, means sickness or bad news for the mistress of the house.

17. The burning of the kitchen means the loss of the cook, or one or more of the servants.

18. Complete destruction of the shop by fire means loss of possessions.

19. The destruction of the front windows by fire portends the loss of a male relative ; the back windows threaten the same event in respect of a female relative.

20. The burning of doors means great misfortune for one of the family—possibly the dreamer himself.

21. To dream that the bedposts are on fire but are not consumed means that the male children will be fortunate.

22. The destruction of the upper part of the house by fire denotes loss of goods, loss of a law-case, or loss of friends.

23. To dream that one is lighting a fire and that it takes light at once, signifies the birth of fortunate children, who will do honour to their mother. The lighting of a lamp or candle carries the same meaning.

24. If it is a married woman who lights either, this shews that she is with child and will be happily delivered of a child, whose life will be fortunate.

25. To dream of lighting a fire with great difficulty and that it goes out at once announces loss and vexation to the housewife and to the dreamer also.

26. To see a house entirely burnt down foretells loss, illness, or great vexation to the owner ; to see a town so destroyed denotes famine, war or pestilence therein.

27. Weariness, injury, slander and loss of friends or at law are prognosticated when the sleeper sees his clothes consumed by fire.

28. The destruction of harvested wheat by fire means an epidemic disease ; but if it should be on fire without being consumed, fertility and plenty may be expected by the dreamer.

29. To see oneself on fire and suffering thereby signifies envy, displeasure, wrath or quarrelling.

30. To dream that one is carrying a torch of lighted straw in a public place signifies honour and success in business.

31. To dream of burning one's finger betokens envy and evil.

B.—The Presages of Air

1. Those who dream that the air is serene and clear will be loved and esteemed by everyone; their enemies and those who envy them will seek reconciliation.

2. People who are accustomed to dream about air are considered to be of sanguine temperament.

3. To see the air pure and cloudless shews that what has been lost or stolen will be recovered, victory will be obtained over enemies, any pending lawsuit gained, the dreamer will be loved by all, and if he is about to travel, he will have a good journey or voyage.

4. To see the air disturbed, cloudy and darkened, forebodes sadness, sickness, melancholy and difficulties in business—in a word, the opposite of all that is announced by clear air.

5. To dream of breathing soft and warm air indicates that the life and habits of the sleeper are pure, peaceable and pleasant, that the business and journeys undertaken by him will succeed to the height of his wishes.

6. To see rain falling gently, without storm or high wind, promises gain in husbandry.

7. The opposite of this spells the opposite in husbandry, with loss and damage of goods to merchants.

8. To dream of long, heavy rains, hail, tempest and lightning signifies ambitions, fatigues, dangers and losses. For poor people, however, it indicates repose.

9. To see snow and ice in winter means nothing ; it may well be the remembrance of yesterday. But when it is not in the winter, good harvest and all plenty are foreshadowed in husbandry. On the other hand, for merchants and business men it intimates hindrance in commerce and in journeys or voyages. For soldiers it may mean good luck, or alternatively uncertainty in their enterprises.

10. To see hail in dream portends trouble and sadness : it may also mean that the most secret and hidden things will be made manifest.

11. To see a thunderbolt fall close by one in still weather signifies that the dreamer will have to take flight, perhaps even to leave his country. This is the case especially with people in high positions. If the bolt falls on one's head, or on houses, it spells danger.

C.—Presages of Fire in Heaven

1. To see a great blaze in the sky denotes aggression on the part of enemies, as also poverty, desolation and famine. Enemies will come from the quarter whence the fire descends. If it is darting fire, falling in several places, the sign is still more unfavourable.

2. To see flaming torches or branches and trees of fire coming down from heaven means war, quarrels, sterility, and the dreamer is menaced with a wound on the head, or other great danger.

3. To see a still, pure and bright fire in heaven is a menace to some prince or distinguished noble.

D.—The Presages of Water

1. Those who are accustomed to dream of water and that they are immersed therein are of phlegmatic disposition; they may be subject to inflammations and colds.

2. To see very clear and quiet river-water is a good augury, especially for travellers, litigants and judges.

3. To see it disturbed means that one is threatened by someone in a high place, or may fall into disgrace with one's master. Litigants will be in difficulties and likely to be judged wrongly.

4. To dream that one is in a rapid river and cannot get out threatens danger for the dreamer, or sickness, or a protracted lawsuit.

5. To dream that one is swimming in a great river signifies imminent peril.

6. To see a clear river gliding past one's chamber prognosticates the coming of some wealthy and generous person, who will bring profit to the dreamer; but if the water is troubled and seems to be damaging the furniture of the room, this means turmoil and disorder, occasioned by enemies of those who dwell in the house.

7. A rich man who dreams that a clear stream is running near his house will soon be in possession of some lucrative and honourable employment, and will be the mainstay of the unfortunate.

8. To see a stream of troubled water signifies loss and damage by fire, lawsuits or enemies.

9. To see a well full of excellent water, in a meadow, is a favourable sign: he who dreams it will make good purchases; he will marry very soon, if he has not done so already, and will have good and obedient children.

10. To see a well overflowing with water predicts loss of goods, or some great misfortune which will befall a relation of the dreamer. In the case of a woman, she is menaced with the loss of part of her property.

11. To dream of a small pond means that a man will be loved by a beautiful woman; but if it is a woman who dreams, she will obtain that which she desires.

12. To be in a boat on a river, lake or pond, where the water is clear, is a sign of joy, prosperity and success in business or occupation.

13. To see streams or fountains of clear, running water presages the rapid cure of a sick dreamer; but if the water is foul or disturbed, this signifies slow recovery.

14. If a young man dreams that he is drawing clear water from a well, it signifies that he will be married presently to a beautiful girl, who will bring him a dowry. But if the water is troubled he will experience difficulty in his courtship.

15. If he dreams that he is giving others to drink from clear well water, this bears witness that he will enrich them; but if the water is troubled, he will prove a cause of loss to them.

16. To dream that one's brook, pool or spring is dried up presages impaired fortune.

17. To dream of water springing up in a place which is unlikely to all appearance promises anxieties, care and affliction.

18. To dream that one draws such water means that the evil fortune will continue for a longer period.

19. To dream that such water ceases to flow means an end of the trouble.

20. To drink warm water announces mischance occasioned by enemies ; the consequent inconvenience will be more or less in proportion to the warmth of the water. Cold water presages good things ; warm or boiling water things that are evil.

21. To see a bath means pain or affliction.

22. To dream of taking a bath and finding it too hot means displeasure and affliction occasioned by relatives. Here also the amount of trouble is regulated by the temperature of the water.

23. To dream of undressing without entering the bath means that the distress to come will be transient.

24. To dream of taking a bath and finding it too cold has the same significance as the opposite extreme ; but if it is temperate, the omen is good.

25. To dream of carrying water in a broken vessel, which cannot contain it, denotes loss and other damage, deception on the part of those who have been entrusted with our goods and money, or robbery by an unknown person.

26. If the water so drawn is not lost, the possessions will be saved with difficulty ; if part is spilt, a partial loss may be expected.

27. If the dreamer buries vessel and water in the ground, a substantial loss is likely.

28. To be given in sleep a glass full of water portends that the dreamer will soon

be married and that his wife will bear him children. Glass always signifies wife or woman; water means abundance, increase and multiplication.

29. If the glass is broken it denotes the loss of several friends.

30. If a preacher dreams that he gives his congregation clear water to drink, this means that the word of God will come forth from his lips and will be the instrument of their salvation.

31. If the water is clouded, he will fail to turn their hearts.

32. To dream of spilling water in one's own house foreshews loss and affliction, the extent of these being in proportion to the quantity of water.

E.—Presages of Life at Sea

1. He who dreams that he is on board ship, and is neither nervous nor otherwise disturbed, will have joy in the success of his affairs; but if the water is stirred by tempest he may look for the opposite.

2. To be on a boat or ship which seems about to founder is a sign of peril, unless the dreamer is in captivity, when it will be a token of coming liberty.

3. To see an anchor signifies safety and certain hope.

4. To dream of ship's rigging betokens

news of debtors or of persons in one's employment.

5. To see the ocean blue and rippling slightly signifies joy and means of success in business.

6. If the sea is utterly becalmed it means delay and protraction.

7. If it is tossed by tempest there is promise of affliction, loss and adversity.

8. To dream of falling into water or the sea, and then to awake with a start, means that the sleeper will be freed with much difficulty from enemies and envious people.

F.—The Presages of Earth

1. He who dreams that he has been given a pleasant piece of ground will have a handsome wife, whose good looks will correspond to the beauty of the land which has become his own in sleep.

2. If it is a spacious area, having gardens, springs, meadows, coppices and abundant orchard, this means that his wife will be pure and prudent, as well as beautiful, and that they will have handsome children.

3. To see the land covered with wheat bespeaks money and profit, with needful care and toil.

4. To see it covered with vegetables means trouble and affliction.

5. To see it covered with millet foretells

great wealth, wealth acquired without difficulty and with joy in the winning.

6. When these dreams are experienced by a wise man, they promise riches and contentment of the mind.

7. To see black earth forecasts sadness, melancholy and credulous weakness.

8. To dream that the earth trembles signifies danger in business-matters.

9. To dream of a great earthquake means that the king or government of the country will perform some public act which will gratify all the people.

10. A slight earthquake presages loss by a lawsuit affecting the house in which the dreamer is sleeping.

11. To dream that walls, doors and roofs collapse in consequence of an earthquake denotes ruination for the owners of the building.

12. If a king or prince dreams that his palace or throne is cast down by an earthquake, he may expect great adversity.

13. To dream that a mountain has fallen into a plain means the downfall of some great peer or noble.

14. To dream that a town of our acquaintance is engulfed by an earthquake is a sign of war and famine; but if the town is unknown to the dreamer the nation to which it belongs will perish through the same causes.

15. To kiss the earth means sorrow and humiliation.

16. To dream of falling into a great ditch, or down a precipice, portends (*a*) great injuries, (*b*) serious danger, or (*c*) that our possessions are menaced by fire through the action of an incendiary.

17. To dream that one is in the meadows is a good sign for agriculturists and shepherds, but it prognosticates an impediment in business for other persons.

18. To dream that one is travelling along a good road, and one that is straight and pleasant, signifies joy, prosperity, success; but a bad road is to be interpreted in the opposite sense.

G.—Presages of Vegetation

I. Flowers

1. To hold and inhale the scent of flowers in their proper season means joy, pleasure, and consolation.

2. But if they are out of season: (*a*) White flowers mean impediment in respect of designs and failure in enterprises; (*b*) Yellow flowers mean less serious impediments; (*c*) Red flowers mean that either impediments are slight or that success may be expected.

3. To hold and inhale the scent of roses in season is a good sign for everyone, except those who are ill or are in hiding through fear.

These are (*a*) in danger of recovering slowly and (*b*) of being found out.

4. The opposite of all this is to be understood if the roses are out of season, so therefore while it is a bad omen in general, it promises quick recovery to the sick and a safe asylum for those desiring concealment.

5. To dream of lilies out of season is a pledge of hopes realised.

6. If a woman should dream of laurel, olive, and palm-trees it means that she will bear children, supposing that she is already married.

7. If they are seen in dream by a maiden, it is a sign of her speedy marriage.

8. If they are seen in dream by a man, they denote friendship, joy, prosperity, abundance and great success in undertakings.

II. The Herb-Garden

1. To dream of smelling sweet marjoram, hyssop, rosemary, sage and herbs of this kind presages toil, sadness and weakness, except for medical men, and it is favourable in their case.

2. To dream of eating or smelling herbs of strong scent—radishes, garlic, onions, leeks and so forth—augurs the disclosure of hidden things and quarrels with servants.

3. To dream of herbs which are used in salads and other vegetables which can be eaten uncooked—lettuce, sorrel and purs-

lain—signifies afflictions and difficulties in business.

4. To eat medicinal herbs, like bugloss, fumitory and borage, promises liberation from weariness and expedition in business affairs.

5. To dream of eating cabbages, colewort or kale foretells vexation.

6. Turnips and cucumbers symbolise vain hopes.

7. Some of the herbalists have ruled that if sick people dream of eating melons and cucumbers, this is a prediction of their recovery.

III. Wheat and other Cereals

1. To see ears of harvested corn in sleep and to pluck some of them typifies profit and riches.

2. To see much corn in sheaves predicts an abundance of good things and benefit for the dreamer.

3. To see a few sheaves only means dearth and necessity.

4. To dream of eating white wheaten bread portends profit to those who are rich, but detriment to the poor.

5. To dream of eating black bread means profit to the poor and loss to those who are rich.

6. To dream of eating a barley-stew is a sign of gain and profit.

7. To see a barn full of corn is a pledge of marriage with a rich woman, success in a suit at law, inheritance of landed estate, wealth gained by trading, gift or otherwise, as well as feasts and rejoicings.

8. To dream of eating well-cooked peas denotes felicity and great acceleration in business things.

9. To eat beans in sleep denotes noise and dissension.

10. To dream of lentils signifies corruption.

11. To dream of rice signifies abundance, or obstruction.

12. To dream of dry millet means want and poverty.

13. To see or eat mustard-seed is a bad sign, except for doctors, to whom the dream is favourable.

IV. Trees and Fruits

1. To see a fine oak in dream promises wealth, profit and long life.

2. To see an olive-tree bearing olives denotes peace, mildness, concord, freedom, dignity and the enjoyment of lawful things desired by the heart.

3. To dream of picking up fallen olives signifies pain and labour.

4. To see a laurel is the sign of victory and pleasure, and in the case of a married man it promises some inheritance through the wife.

5. To see a cypress denotes vexations, afflictions and delay in business matters.

6. To see a pine, medlar, or service-tree spells idleness.

7. To see apple-trees and eat sweet apples means joy, pleasure and recreation, above all for women and maids.

8. To eat almonds, walnuts and hazel-nuts is an omen of troubles and difficulties.

9. To see figs in their season is a sign of joy and pleasure, but it is the opposite if they are out of season.

10. To see a vine typifies abundance, riches and fruitfulness.

11. To eat ripe grapes speaks of joy and profit.

12. To see and partake of oranges threatens wounding, pains and vexations.

13. Mulberries have the same significance.

14. To see and to eat peaches or apricots in season is a pledge of contentment, health and enjoyment.

15. If they are out of season they speak of vain hopes and failure in business.

16. To see and to eat ripe pears foretells joy and pleasure, but it is the reverse if they are sour and wild.

17. To see a mulberry-tree in dream means a wealth of good things, including a promise of children.

18. To find hidden nuts means the discovery of a treasure.

19. To see mulberry-trees, almond-trees and to partake of their fruit, is a sign of joy, consolation and diversion; but if they are withered, barren, leafless, fallen, burnt or blasted by lightning, they foretell weariness, fear, displeasure and suffering.

20. To gather the fruit of a pomegranate-tree means that the dreamer will be enriched by a man of wealth; but if the fruit is not ripe it denotes illness or trouble occasioned by the wicked.

21. To dream of gathering fruits and finding them rotten is a sign of adversity or the loss of children.

22. To dream that one has climbed a great tree speaks of approaching elevation to some degree of dignity and that others will be under our rule.

23. To dream of falling from a tree and being scratched by brambles, or hurt in some other manner, portends the loss of favour with influential persons.

H.—Presages of Birds and Insects

1. To dream of an eagle in a high place, or flying through the mid-heaven is good for those who are starting on some great undertaking, especially in military affairs.

2. To dream of an eagle swooping down on one's head is a sign of illness.

3. To dream of being carried off by an eagle has the same import.

4. If a woman gives birth to an eagle in dream, this predicts that she will bear a child who will attain greatness and will rule others.

5. To see a dead eagle means loss to those in high places and gain for those in poverty.

6. To see birds of prey or those used in hawking signifies increase of fortune and honour for the rich and some change of position for the poor.

7. To see a raven in sleep is a bad sign and above all for a husband, who may have cause for grave self-reproach. In the case of a wife or woman it prognosticates deep affliction.

8. To see a rook or carrion-crow signifies despatch in business matters.

9. To see a starling portends a slight displeasure.

10. To see doves is a good sign: there will be joy and pleasure in the house and success in business.

11. To see cranes or storks flocking through the air means the approach of enemies or envious relations. In winter they denote bad weather.

12. To see two storks together promises marriage and birth of children, who will be good and profitable to their parents.

13. To see a swan is the pledge of coming gaiety and the revelation of secret things; it also means health to the dreamer.

14. To see a singing swan is of evil augury.

15. To see a swallow is the gage of a good wife, good news and of blessing on one's own home.

16. To see a nightingale has the same meanings.

17. To see bees signifies gain for the country people and loss for the rich.

18. To dream that bees have made their honey in some part of the house speaks of dignity, eloquence and success in business.

19. To dream of being stung by flies, especially wasps, portends weariness and troubles caused by the envious.

20. To see many birds foretells assemblies and lawsuits.

21. To hear a cock crow announces joy and prosperity.

22. To see two cocks fighting means feud and warfare.

23. To see a peacock means a beautiful and wealthy wife, who is a favourite with the great of this world.

24. To see a hen with its chickens presages loss and damage.

25. To see a capon or hear a hen crow is significant of sadness and weariness.

26. To see partridges is an omen of dealing with unscrupulous, ungrateful and evil women.

27. Quails are prophetic of bad news by

sea, disputes, bickerings, larcenies, ambushes and treason.

28. All night-birds—screech-owl, common owl, or bat—are of evil augury; those who see them in dreams should enter into no new undertaking on the following day.

29. To dream of eggs promises gain; but if they are in very great numbers, anxiety and litigation may be expected.

30. Grasshoppers, may-bugs, crickets and cicadas signify great talkers, bad musicians, and needy people who plunder the country-side. This dream offers no good prospect to the sleeper, at least during the first day following.

31. To see scorpions or caterpillars presages trouble occasioned by the envious.

32. To dream of earth-worms denotes that enemies are seeking to take us by surprise and injure us.

I.—Presages from Reptiles and Fishes

1. To dream of a dragon means a meeting with some influential person, with one's master, or with a magistrate.

2. To see a serpent twisting and coiling denotes that one has enemies: it stands for hate and sickness.

3. To see a serpent otherwise signifies treason on the part of a woman.

4. To dream that one destroys a serpent

signifies victory over enemies and jealous people.

5. To see basilisks and lizards promises loss or opposition arising from secret enemies.

6. Frogs signify flatterers, babblers and ignorant persons.

7. To dream of catching large fish is a token of profit in proportion to the quantity taken.

8. To catch small fish is a mark of coming sadness.

9. To see fish of many colours promises recovery to the sick, but to those who are well it means injuries, quarrels, or pains.

10. To eat big fish in a dream is an omen of inflammation, colds and depression.

11. To dream of fishing-nets is a sign of rain or some other change in the weather.

12. To see dead fish in the sea is a portent of vain hopes.

13. If a woman who is with child dreams of giving birth to a fish, her actual offspring will be a fine child who will attain length of days.

K.—Presages of Quadrupeds

1. He who sees a lion in his sleep will speak either to his sovereign or to some illustrious soldier.

2. To dream of fighting with a lion is the pledge of a struggle with some courageous

opponent; and if a victory is gained in the sleep-life, it will be gained in the life of day.

3. To ride on the back of a lion signifies princely protection, or at least that of an influential person.

4. To be afraid of a lion in sleep is to have merited the royal displeasure, or that of some great person.

5. He who dreams of eating lion's flesh will be enriched and covered with honours.

6. To dream of finding the hide, liver or marrow of a lion means that one in high place will obtain the treasures of his enemies and that an ordinary person will grow rich in a short time.

7. If a king dreams that he is carried off bound by a lion, he will be made a prisoner.

8. If he dreams that a lioness and her cubs are in his palace, this signifies that the queen and the royal children will cause him much satisfaction.

9. Dreams about leopards are of the same significance as those concerning lions, allowance being made for the craft of the former beasts and for the generous qualities ascribed to the latter.

10. To dream of an elephant stands for fear and danger, but the testimony of interpreters differs on this point. It is said also to denote a rich man who may bring fortune to the dreamer.

11. To dream of riding on an elephant may be a presage of approaching illness.

12. To dream of giving food and drink to an elephant means entrance into the service of some great personage, to the profit of the dreamer.

13. To see a bear signifies an enemy who is wealthy and powerful, but awkward, ridiculous and insolent.

14. To dream of overcoming a wolf means triumph over an avaricious, cruel and disloyal foe.

15. To be bitten by a wolf has the contrary meaning.

16. To dream of combating a fox indicates a dispute with a crafty and acute enemy.

17. He who dreams that he has a tame fox at home will fall in love with an evil woman and be a slave to her; or alternatively, he will trust a domestic who will abuse his goodness.

18. To see lynxes, martens or weasels will bear a similar interpretation.

19. To dream of chasing or capturing a wild boar means hunting or cornering an enemy possessed of that animal's qualities, which are rage and cruelty.

20. To dream of carrying the head of a wild boar recently taken in the chase means speedy triumph over our most powerful enemy.

21. When swine are beheld in dream they

stand for idle and good for nothing people, who seek to live at their ease by preying on others. They also represent misers.

22. To dream about dogs that belong to us denotes faith, courage and affection in friends.

23. To dream of strange dogs signifies dangerous enemies.

24. To dream that a barking dog is rending our clothes gives warning of an enemy in some lower walk of life who is slandering and trying to disgrace us.

25. The cat is supposed to stand for a clever thief, and to dream of fighting with a cat or destroying one means casting a thief into prison or in some way putting an end to his activities.

26. To dream of having a cat's skin means that the thief's spoil will come into our hands.

27. To dream of being scratched by a cat signifies illness or afflictions.

28. To dream of monkeys is significant of malicious, weak, strange and unknown enemies.

29. To dream of killing a stag and taking its horns and hide means inheritance from an aged person, or the defeat of deceptive, cowardly and retreating enemies.

30. To see ourselves owners of much cattle, horses and so forth, signifies wealth and plenty.

31. To dream of being butted by a ram threatens punishment by law.

32. An ass seen in sleep means a good servant who is profitable to his master, or else an inept and ignorant fellow.

33. To see a mule in dream is a promise of contrariety.

34. To dream of an ox is to dream of a faithful servant.

35. To dream of a bull signifies some person of importance, and as the bull does good or otherwise to us in our sleep so will his representative in waking life.

36. It is always of good augury to see or get possession of a horse and also to be riding on one.

37. To dream of riding a fine horse, full of courage and activity, and well harnessed, means marriage with a handsome woman, wealthy and of high birth; but this is on condition that the horse is understood to be ours. If it belongs to another, joy, honour and possessions will come to us through an unknown woman.

38. He who dreams of riding horse or mare over a hard and rugged road, without the animal stumbling, will obtain honour, dignity and renown.

39. To be carried by a long-tailed horse means reinforcement of friends who will help our enterprises.

40. If the horse limps in our dream, obstacles will interfere with our design.

41. To dream that someone is riding one

of our horses against our will denotes an attempt to seduce one of our servants.

42. Other interpreters say that to ride a bold and fiery horse is a pledge that the dreamer will be honoured by the public and esteemed by the great.

43. If the rider spurs such a horse and has him fully under control he will be advanced in offices and dignities : his honours will be in proportion to his performance.

44. In the dreams of kings, a white horse has reference to the person of the coming queen and promises that she will be beautiful and good.

45. A black horse in the same case refers to a rich but wicked woman.

46. To dream that a young, frisky and well-harnessed mare comes into one's house signifies speedy marriage with a fair, young and wealthy lady, by whom our happiness will be insured. But if the mare have no saddle and is not good to look at, a female servant is signified, or a mistress who will bring nothing.

47. To be riding through the streets of a large town, followed by a cheering crowd, presages that the dreamer will be at the head of some popular faction.

L.—Presages of Perfumes

1. To dream that one's head is perfumed with oils, essences or powders signifies great

self-esteem and pride exhibited to others. In the case of a woman she will glory in the exercise of power.

2. To dream of being adorned and to think that one is looking at one's best speaks of coming danger, through illness or otherwise.

3. The easterns say that to dream of being perfumed means that we shall be esteemed by our neighbours and agreeable to all about us.

4. He who dreams of exuding bad odours will soon prove hateful to others.

5. He who dreams that he has been presented with aromatic or scented waters will have good news in proportion to the quality and extent of the gifts received in sleep; he will make a substantial gain and acquire honours.

6. He who dreams of distributing scents to his friends will have news advantageous to himself and those about him.

M.—Presages of Wounds

1. To dream of being wounded by a sword and like to die thereof signifies that the sleep-victim will have pleasures and benefactions from the hand of the person who has appeared to maim him, and that they will be in proportion to the number and severity of the blows.

2. To be so wounded by a person in high place, and especially by a ruler of the land, means benefits from that person in the proportion above mentioned.

3. If a woman is wounded in dream or strikes with the sword in self-defence, or in some other good cause, she will receive honours and, if she be married, will give birth to a male child.

4. If a royal person, or some one in high command, is struck upstanding by sword or knife, and if the attacking party be one of mean estate, the dreamer is in danger of being killed or cast down from his high position.

N.—Presages of Hair

1. If a man dreams that his hair is long like a woman's, this denotes poltroonery and effeminacy, or otherwise, deception by a woman.

2. To see a woman without hair signifies famine, poverty and sickness.

3. To see a hairless man has the opposite meaning.

4. To see mixed hair is an omen of pain and weariness, sometimes of injuries and quarrels.

5. To see very black hair, which is also short and frizzled, promises suffering and sadness.

6. To dream of combing one's hair and

being unable to draw the comb through announces long toil and a suit at law.

7. To see a head with the hair well-dressed means friendship and freedom from bad business.

8. He who dreams that his beard or head is being shaved will be in danger of losing a substantial part of his possessions, or of falling ill, or of losing one of whom he is fond.

9. To see hair fall off signifies weariness and loss of goods.

10. The soldier who dreams that his hair is very good and abundant will become terrible to his enemies—supposing that he is a person in command—will acquire a great reputation and will subject many provinces.

11. To dream that one's hair has whitened means that possessions will diminish, almost to a vanishing point.

12. To dream that it has grown longer and darker means increase of honours and riches.

13. To dream that the hair of one's beard is cut or torn off is generally of evil omen and especially as regards loss of goods.

14. To dream that one's beard has grown unusually means increase of money.

15. To dream that one's hair has become thinner is a sign of poverty and affliction.

O.—Presages of the Visage

I. The Forehead

1. To dream that one has a broad forehead symbolises a broad mind, and if it is also high, this is a mark of good judgment, as well as of power and wealth.

2. To dream that one has a front of brass testifies to irreconcilable hatred of enemies.

3. To dream that one's head is broken or wounded gives warning of riches discovered and in danger of being lost. It denotes also fear and apprehension.

4. To dream that one has a bulky and fleshy forehead means facility of speech, force and constancy.

II. Complexion

1. To dream that one has a wife with a graceful head and fair countenance promises joy, contentment and safety.

2. If a woman sees a handsome man in her sleep, the meaning is similar.

3. To see an unknown man of brown complexion signifies honour and glory.

4. To see a very dark woman threatens a dangerous illness.

5. To see an unknown woman with long and beautiful hair is a promise of friendship, joy and prosperity.

6. To see a fresh and radiant face is a sign of friendship.

7. To see an emaciated and pallid face portends weariness and poverty.

III. Eyebrows and Eyelashes

1. To dream that one's eyebrows and lashes have grown thicker and more beautiful is a sign of being generally honoured and esteemed, fortunate in love and destined to become rich.

2. To dream that they have come off carries the contrary meaning.

IV. The Nose

1. To dream that one's nose has grown larger is a promise of wealth, power, increased sagacity and of welcome on the part of the great.

2. To dream that one has no nose signifies the opposite of this.

3. To dream that one has two noses means strife and discord.

4. To dream of one's nose becoming so large that it is deformed and hideous to view promises prosperity and abundance, but not popularity.

5. To dream that one's nose is obstructed, so that nothing can be smelt, is to be in danger of deception by a friend or servant.

6. In the case of a woman, she must be on her guard, or she may be betrayed.

V. The Ears

1. To dream of being all ears means that we shall win the friendship of servants and those about us, that we shall be served and obeyed faithfully.

2. To dream of washing the ears bears the same interpretation as the above.

3. To dream that our ears are hung with wheat is a sign of inheritance from relations.

4. To dream of having ass's ears signifies service.

5. To dream of having lion's ears, or those of some other savage beast, promises treason on the part of enemies and jealous people.

6. If any one dreams that his ears are larger and finer than usual, he will find that the person to whom he has communicated his secrets will attain honour and prosperity.

7. To have an ear wounded or cloven in dream portends our betrayal by someone belonging to our family or circle and to whom our secrets have been entrusted.

8. To dream that an ear has been cut off completely means that we shall be deprived of the friendship of those who are near to us.

9. To dream that one's ears are stopped up intimates a change in our plans and that we shall deceive those who depend upon us.

10. In the case of a woman, she is in danger of seduction.

VI. The Eyes

1. He who dreams of losing his sight will not keep his promise: otherwise, he is in danger of illness, of seeing his friends no more, or of his child falling ill.

2. To dream that one's eyes are bleary means the commission of a grave fault, followed by repentance. It may mean also the loss of part of one's property.

3. It is good to dream that our sight is keen and clear; it is a promise of prosperity in enterprise.

4. To dream that our sight is short and dim signifies want of cash and failure in business.

VII. The Mouth

1. To dream that our mouth has grown larger means greater wealth in the house.

2. To dream that one's mouth is closed tightly and cannot be opened is a sign of approaching illness.

3. A bad taste in the mouth and a bad odour may signify falling into general contempt and being hated by one's servants.

VIII. The Cheeks

1. To have plump and vermilion cheeks is a good sign in dream: it means prosperity in business things and in the general sense.

2. To dream that one's cheeks are thin and pallid has the opposite significance.

A CONCISE ALPHABETICAL LIST OF PERSONS AND SUBJECTS IN DREAM

A

Abandonment—of one's house—Gain; of one's position—Loss by bad faith; of one's wife—Assured felicity.

Abbess, or Nun—Safety, protection.

Academy—of learning—Weariness; of arms—Danger; of amusements—Snares.

Accuse—to—Weariness; to be accused—Joy.

Adoption—Crosses.

Adoration—Peace of soul.

Adultery—Strife and dole.

Adventure—to hear account of—Chatter, scandal.

Adversary—Contrarieties.

Adversity—Trouble, warfare.

Air—if clear—Fortune; if clouded—Danger.

Apples—Concubinage.

Apricots—Misfortune; if out of season—Felicity.

Angel—Great honours.

Anchor—Security in hope.

Appetite—to have a great—Estrangement from relatives or friends.

Apartment—Enjoyments, comfort.

Assassin—Unexpected wealth.

Asylum—to seek—Misery; to find—A protector.

Ass—Evil society; to hear one bray—Damage; to see donkey's ears—Scandal.

B

Ball—Death of a neighbour or acquaintance.

Bank—Safety.

Basket—Promise of a child; approaching demand in marriage.

Bailiff—Sinister neighbours; unexpected misfortunes.

Bath—Marriage; cold—False measures; in stagnant water—Bad news.

Bat—Fire.

Bear—Danger.

Beard—large—Terror; black—Success; white—Dignities; to cut—Loss.

Bed—to sleep in—Peril; to see one well made—Guarantee of relations.

Beer—to drink—Loss of time.

Beggars—Internal pains.

Bolts—Difficulties in domestic arrangements.
Bellows—A faithful and sure wife.
Bells—to see—An elevated position ; to hear—Bad news.
Betting Man—An unlucky neighbour.
Billiards—Loss ; to play—Fatigue.
Birds—Profits, pleasure, success.
Blood—Contagious disease.
Blow—the fire—Moral corruption ; blow out the light—Attempt on conjugal happiness.
Bone—Death.
Bonnet—of cotton—A ridiculous husband ; of silk—A cold.
Books—Weariness ; holy—Indisposition ; to write books—Loss of time and money.
Breasts—full—Abundance ; barren—Misery.
Bridal—Obsequies.
Brigands—A visit from a bailiff.
Burial—Repose secured ; burial alive—Great fortune.
Butterfly—A volatile and fickle husband.

C

Cabin—Tranquil happiness.
Café—Conspiracy made void.
Camel—Riches.
Candle — if lighted — Prosperous business ; extinguished — Trickery ; of wax—Widowhood ; if lighted—A second marriage.
Canticle—Sweet folly.
Cards—Aberration and cheating.
Carriage—one's own—Ambition ; to descend from—Loss of employment.
Cart—Despair.
Castle—Great fortune.
Cat—Duplicity ; asleep—Danger run.
Cavalier—Fall.
Caves—Clouded futurity.
Chains—Dejection ; if broken—Joy.
Chase—A lost law-case.
Cemetery—News of a death.
Cheeks—if plump—Cause for gaiety ; if hollow—Abstinence.
Cherries—Pleasure ; Cherry-stones—Difficulties.
Chemise—if soiled—Shame ; in rags—Misery.
Chimney—Sadness ; with a fire—Joy.
Chocolate—Health and joy.
Cistern—A bad proposition.
Church—to build one—Divine Love ; to visit one—Beneficence, honourable conduct ; to pray therein—Consolation and joy ; to be distracted therein—Envy, sin ; to be asleep therein—Change of habits.

Childbirth—Abundance ; birth of an animal—Riddance of an enemy.
Clock—Immorality.
Cloth—A substantial gain.
Clouds—Projects in the air.
Clyster—Public scandal.
Coals—Stamped paper.
Cock—Pride.
Comb—to—Forgetfulness of injuries.
Comedy—to read one—Trickery; to see one—Pleasure shared.
Cows—if fat—Abundance ; if lean—Distress.
Country—Possible ruin ; Voyage.
Crab—Retreat.
Cradle—Sudden death.
Crown—of iron—Suffering ; of flowers—Honours and dignities ; of gold—Punished pride.
Cypress—Death of a friend.

D

Dance—Loss of money.
Daughters of Joy—Good society and gain.
Death—A fair future.
Devil—An offer of marriage.
Débris—An unexpected gain.
Deluge—Loss of harvest or vintage, disaster.
Dentist—Falsehood, trickery.
Deserter—News of an absent person.
Diamond—Great projects.
Dice—to cast and win—An inheritance coming from a relation.
Discord—Marriage at hand.
Distaff—Great misfortune.
Ditch—to cross—Prudence in business ; to fall in—Bad management.
Dispute—among women—Discord ; among friends—Uncertainty and peril.
Doctor—Ill omen.
Dog—Fidelity ; barking—Death ; to coax—Friendship ; to be bitten by—Damage.
Drown—oneself—Prompt fortune.
Dumb—person—Tranquillity in home affairs.
Dwarf—A ridiculous attack.
Duel—Home discord, or between friends ; dangerous rivalry ; uncertainty and peril.

E

Eagle—flying—Satisfied ambition; to eat—Fall; dead—A tumble.

Earth—Abundance and riches.

Earthquake—Peril.

Echo—Deafness.

Eclipse—of the sun—Substantial loss; of the moon—Trivial loss.

Eel—alive—Shame; dead—Despair.

Elephant—Certain defence.

Eggs—Lucrative employment.

Embrace—of parents or friends—Treason; of a stranger—Voyage at hand.

Embroidery—Minute work.

Enemies—to talk with—Saving mistrust; to conquer—Gain in lawsuit; to play with—Disadvantage; to be seized by—Embarrassment, negligence, idleness; to conceive hatred of—Pain and reverse of fortune.

Excrement—A cordial welcome; to sweep up—Expulsion from the paternal house.

Executioner—Unforeseen death.

Exile—Political disaster.

Eyebrows—Terrifying news.

Eyes—Agreement over business, happiness, success.

F

Face—if beautiful—Honour, long life, happiness; if ugly—Vexation.

Fan—Secret slander.

Fall—to—An attempt against one's honour.

Father—Birth of a child.

Feasting—Deceitful illusion, joy of short duration, ruin of temperament.

Feet—if white—Travel; if soiled—Damage; to wash one's own—Going back into oneself; to kiss—Disease of the stomach.

Fire—to fall therein—Danger; if bright—Fortune; if extinguished—Misery.

Figures—Cavil and legal process.

Fish—in the water—Pleasures; in the frying-pan—An adventurous situation; to fish with the line—Patience badly rewarded.

Flowers—if fresh—Fortune; if withered—Reverses; if artificial—Dupery.

Flutes—Pleasures of debauchery.

Fool—Perfect happiness.

Footstool—Public debauch.

Forest—Laxity of morals.
Fountain—Disease of the bladder.
Friend—Discord ; to leave one—Quarrel.
Frog—Ridiculous pride.
Fruits—if fresh—Pleasure ; if damaged—a frivolous woman.
Fox—Seduction by an inferior, offspring of adultery.

G

Gallantry—Mystification and pleasantry.
Gallows—Exalted dignities.
Gammon—Shameful vices.
Garment—Distress ; to cast one off—A secret defect.
Game—Inclination towards small faults.
Garden—Promises of future delights.
Girdle—if new—Honour ; if broken—Damage ; if worn—Toil, pain ; if golden—Gain to the wearer ; if silver—A somewhat smaller gain.
God—Elevation.
Gold—Bad speculation ; to give—Stupidity ; to find—Misery ; to lose—Profit.
Gooseberries—if red—A good connection ; if white—Pleasures shared ; if black—Conjugal infidelity.
Good—to do—Satisfaction, profit ; to possess many goods—Discussion, perhaps sadness to come ; to inherit—Dole.
Goat—nanny—Profit ; if black—Loss.
Gorge—False hopes ; mountain gorge—Hindrance in business.
Great—to be persecuted by—Honour ; to be feasted by—Shame and loss.
Granary—if full—A fruitful marriage ; if empty—Misery and beggary ; if burnt—A very large profit.
Grass—Amorous presages.
Grating—Threatened imprisonment.
Guitar—Sign of mental weakness.

H

Hair—Robust health ; to be covered with—Long life ; woman's hair—Miscarriage.
Hands—Remunerative work ; if dirty—Sickness.
Handsel—Hopes frustrated.
Hanged Man—Ill gotten gain.
Hare—running—Fortune to come ; if entrapped or otherwise caught—Inheritance.
Hatchet—Menace of death.
Hatred—A lawsuit gained.
Hay—Omen of disaster.
Haricots—Pointless criticism.

Herbs—Plenty ; to eat—Ruin.
Hen—Famine ; if large—Abundance.
Health—Declining health.
Hermit—to see one—Treason on the part of a false friend ; to become one—stillness of passion, soothing of infirmities.
Hips—if large—Fecundity, joy, health ; if narrow—separation of body.
Hell—A catastrophe seen from far away.
Heaven—A good sign.
Heritage—An accident without importance.
Hole—Miserly to the end.
Honey—False protestations.
Hook—An omen of being duped.
Hose—if cast aside—Abandonment ; if new—Visit from mother-in-law or step-mother ; in good condition—Success at hand.
Hospital—Distress and abandonment.
House—Feud with all relations and friends.
Hunger—Pressing need ; if satisfied—A chance enjoyment.

I

Ice—Trust ensnared.
Illuminations—False joy followed by tears.
Incendiary Fire—An attack to foresee ; if extinguished—Triumph over enemies.
Inundation—Many misfortunes.
Intoxication—End of an illness.
Iron—Effusion of blood.

J

Jew—Deception, direct or indirect theft ; if he renders some service—Unexpected happiness, success.
Journal—Loss of peace.
Judge—Malice and cruelty ; if the dreamer has some self-reproach—Disculpation ; to exercise the functions of—Weariness.
Justice—to be delivered to—Happiness ; to be liberated by—An intrigue ; to be hounded by—Everything to fear.

K

Kill—An evil sign.
King—Advantages, cuckoldom.
Kiss—the face—Joy ; the earth—Abasement to come.
Knees—to go on—Embarrassment in business, troubles, an inconvenient position ; also humility, devotion.
Knife—Separation.

L

Ladder—to climb—Elevation; to descend—A plan renounced; to fall from—Failure.

Lamb—in meadow—Pleasure; to carry one—Goodness; to buy—Disillusion.

Lantern—Confusion and noise; if lighted—Disasters at hand.

Larder—A necessary precaution; on fire—Shameful and inexpressible desires.

Laughter—An apoplectic fit.

Laurel—for men—A glorious sign; for women—Great and fortunate fruitfulness; for girls—Loss of virginity.

Leech—Interested friendship.

Legs—well-shaped—Prosperity; knock-kneed—Difficulties in attaining the desired terms.

Lightning—Success beyond hope.

Linen—if clean—Inward cares; if otherwise—Fatal neglect.

Lion—to overcome—Energy; to fight—An approaching struggle; to kill—A hard victory.

Lock—A theft to fear.

Lover—to have one—Grief; to have many—Profit; to leave one—Consolation.

M

Man—proud—Love dawning; ugly—Trickery; black—Misfortune.

Mantle—Trickery and sham wealth.

Marble—Treason and revenge.

Marriage—A dangerous future.

Matches—An exalted employment.

May-bug—Folly.

Milk—to drink—Great satisfaction; friendship of women; to spill—Loss in trade.

Mill—Rapid fortune.

Mirror—Treason.

Moon—if full—Rejoicing; if waning—Sickness.

Mother—Protection and blessing of heaven.

Mountain—Elevation.

Mouse—Broils with neighbours.

Moustache—Bad diseases, the treatment of which is secret.

Mouth—if large—An enemy beaten; if coarse—Grief.

N

Nails—A slight ailment; of the hands—Dispute, quarrel.

Nakedness—one's own—Confusion; of a woman—Ends fulfilled.

Navel—Guilty thought.

Nest—An illusion lost.
Nettles—Suffering.
Nose—if coarse—Licentious pleasures ; if small—Deception.
Nurse—Good health.

O

Obsequies—A false surprise.
Obscurity—Melancholy, abortive appointment.
Oak—Force and power.
Oculist—A miserable discovery.
Onion—Tears without a serious cause.
Opera—Transient satisfaction.
Osier—Imprisonment.
Ox—Great success ; to see an ox running—A secret repeated.
Oysters—Gluttony ; to eat—Women of evil life.

P

Palliasse—Profits from a bad source.
Pain—Chance and profit.
Palace—Fleeting pleasures mixed with dark cares.
Palm—A token of honour.
Paper—Unexpected news.
Parade—Profitable issue of an affair.
Paradise—An empty promise.
Parents—Immediate protection.
Parrot—An evening at the theatre.
Patrol—Publicity.
Peacock—Foolish pride.
Penknife—Conjugal escapades.
Perfume—if good—Success without stability ; if bad—Prostitution.
Peach—Satisfaction.
Painter—Long life.
Pearls—to thread—Dishonour.
Penalty—Unhoped-for wealth.
Phantoms—Protection.
Pigeons—A favourable destiny.
Pen—Gratified ambition.
Pilgrim—Health and strength.
Pins—Women's spitefulness.
Pomp—Impotent efforts.
Portraits—To be on guard against wiles and witchcraft.
Police—Evil society.
Pond—abounding in fish—Profit ; dried up—Disillusion ; if muddy—Misery.
Precipice—Imbecility.
Pregnancy—A son to be born.

Priest—Always a bad presage, especially for those in prison.
Prison—A timid conscience.
Purse—if full—Vexations, pain, want, avarice ; if empty—Satisfaction, ease.

Q

Quarrel—with a man—Oppression ; with a woman—A pleasure-party.
Question—Happiness, ease, prudence.
Quay—Foresight, isolation from all danger.

R

Radish—A menace of dropsy.
Raisin—Intoxication ; if green—Derangement.
Rats—Falling off of the hair.
Reapers—Gain and success.
Removal—Embarrassment.
Riches—Ambush.
Ring—Alliance.

S

Salmon—Dangers to fear.
Saw—to—Fortune built up by degrees.
Salt—if white—Good conduct ; if gray—Change the speculation.
Seed—to sow—Opulence after hard work.
Sentinel—Pregnancy.
Serpent—Trickery ; if the dreamer kills it—Victory.
Sausage—Sensuality.
Sea—Be on your guard ; to navigate—Great joy ; to fall into—Irreparable misfortune.
Sheep—Abundance, long and fortunate voyage ; if killed—Want.
Shipwreck—Decease of some remote relative.
Shoes—if large—An easy result ; if small—Troublesome labour.
Shroud—Death impending, either for self or others.
Silver—to see—Success ; loss of—Gain ; to count up—Misfortune.
Sign—to receive a—Doubtful intentions.
Sepulchre—Warning of evils to be withstood.
Skate—Mistaken confidence in business.
Skin—Advantageous business.
Sky—Good sign.
Slaughter—Flourishing health.
Sleep—with a man—Conjugal intoxication ; with a man who is not one's husband—Awkwardness and a taste for pleasure ;

with a handsome youth—Care ; with a pretty woman—Mortification ; with a prostitute—Poignant grief.

Smoke—The glory of a day.

Snail—False friendship.

Sneezing—A good chance in business.

Snow—Financial success.

Soldiers—Troubles at hand.

Sorcerer—Abuse of confidence.

Songs—of woman—Tears ; of birds—Scandal, chatter ; of man—False hopes.

Spectacle—Pleasure, marriage, happiness.

Spectre—Slight impediments in coming affair.

Spider—in the evening—Hope, success ; at morning—Vexation ; to kill—Intoxication ; to eat—Vengeance.

Speak—in public—Insolence ; to a woman—Profit ; to an enemy—Domestic dispute.

Stags—Certain profits.

Stairway—Painful prominence.

Stars—An adventurous affair.

Skittles—Deceptive glory ; if turned over—A serious fall.

Starling—Good news.

Statue—Domestic coldness.

Stiletto—Danger of death.

Stockings—if of cotton—Pleasure ; if of silk—Unrestrained joy.

Stone—Traps.

Storm—Imminent danger.

Straw—Prosperity and joy ; if burnt—A good meal.

Sugar—Deceptive appearance of security.

Suicide—A strong resolve.

Sulphur—An attack of jaundice, or an affection of the skin.

Supper—Birth of a fine baby.

Sutler—Fortune by hook or by crook.

Swallow—Successful projects, favoured undertakings.

Stork—Loss by theft.

Swans—Riches and power ; if black—Domestic embroilments ; if they sing—Death.

Swear—Evil habit.

Swim—A flirtation with a fair woman.

Swine—A doleful happening.

Sword—at the side—Defence and victory ; to be struck by —Dangerous wound.

T

Tobacco—Short joy.

Table—Return of health.

Tailor—Bad faith.

Tambourine—False reports, but of no consequence.

Tail—of any animal—Public confusion.
Task—Loss of money or consideration.
Tavern—Pains; if full—consolation.
Teeth—if clean—Good health; if otherwise—A doubtful position; if they seem to be falling out—Family accidents.
Tempest—Separation.
Tents—Disputes between familiar acquaintances.
Theatre—Loss of time.
Theft—Troubles in the head.
Thistle—Hunger and want.
Thorn—Neighbours to avoid.
Thunder—Threatenings.
Tiger—Enmity.
Tillage—An expected reward.
Tomb—to build one—Loss of friends or relatives; to destroy one—Betrothal, marriage; to see one in ruins—Illness, family misfortunes; to fall into one—Misery; to visit one—Regrets.
Tortoise—Slow business.
Torture—Moral corruption.
Travel—Loss of money; on foot—A fall; on horseback—ostentation and ridicule.
Trees—if erect—Success; if fallen—A domestic quarrel; to climb—Desire of attainment, good news.
Trough—if full—A good harvest or profit; if empty—Want.
Trunk—Distress, want.
Turtle—Fidelity and conjugal constancy.
Turnip—A narrow mind.

U

Ulcer—Coming bankruptcy.
Uniform—to see or wear one—Glory, valour.
Usurer—Serious fall.

V

Vampire—Troubled conscience.
Vane—A distinguished person's favour, a frail support.
Virgin—A mind deceived and prone to deception.
Vine—Sweet consolation.
Violet—Modesty.
Violin—Perfect harmony in marriage.
Viper—Treason on the part of a friend, conjugal interference.
Visits—to pay—Tears; to receive—An enviable position; of a doctor—Approaching failure in business.

W

Walk—if slowly—A futile enterprise; with stick in hand—Infirmity; if quickly—Success.

Wall—Impotence; to fall from one—Endless enjoyments and feastings.

Waltz—The dreamer will be led by women.

Wand—Dispute; to break one—A plan collapsed; to beat some one—Sincere friendship.

Wash—Arrangement of affairs.

Wasp—Reconciliation of enemies.

Water—if clear—Success; if troubled—Difficulties.

Well—if deep—Purchase of goods; if foul—Loss of benefits or profits.

Wheat—Abundance, general prosperity.

Will—Inheritance.

Window—to pass by one—Decadence, failure.

Wolf—to chase one—Generosity of heart; to be bitten by one—Coming dupery by friends.

Woman—Weakness, indecision, ill luck; to hear but not see one—Change of place.

Workman—Good business.

Y

Yacht—Omen of a long voyage.

Z

Zebra—A friend of many moods.

Zephyr—Lightness and inconstancy in love.

Zero—Trifling chance or mischance.

Zodiac—To see the Signs in dream shews that one is born to read in the great book of futurity.